The New York Times
♦ BRIDGE SERIES ♥
GRAND SLAMS
♠ ♣

Other books by Alan Truscott include

Official Encyclopedia of Bridge
The Great Bridge Scandal
The New York Times Guide to Practical Bridge
Master Bridge by Question and Answer
Teach Yourself Basic Bidding (with Dorothy Truscott)

The New York Times
♦ BRIDGE SERIES ♥
GRAND SLAMS
♠   ♣

ALAN TRUSCOTT

Times
BOOKS

Library of Congress Cataloging in Publication Data

Truscott, Alan F.
    Grand slams.

    1. Contract bridge—Slams. I. Title.
GV1282.48.T78   1985   795.41'53   84-40647
ISBN 0-8129-6346-6

Designed by Marjorie Anderson
Manufactured in the United States of America
9 8 7 6 5 4 3 2
First Edition

To my wife, Dorothy, and my son, Philip, whose efficient and enthusiastic assistance enabled me to surprise the publishers with an instant book.

Contents

INTRODUCTION

When I first contemplated the possibility of this book, I thought I would have difficulty in finding enough material. It turned out, however, that in my first twenty years as Bridge Editor of *The New York Times*, I described 509 grand slams. In other words, I was at the seven-level twice a month—about the same frequency as many of my readers.

About one third of these columns seemed to have some permanent value, and I had great difficulty in selecting the fifty-five for which there was space. I have deliberately omitted two hands that are already well known: the missed brilliancy by Kantar against Belladonna, which might have changed the result of the 1975 world championship, and Hamman's lead in 1980, which certainly gave the Olympiad title to France.

It would have been easy to collect examples of squeezes, endplays, and other technical marvels. I have not done so, preferring entertainment to education. But there are lessons to be learned, particularly in the field of freak deals, which, I confess, are somewhat over-represented.

The headlines are those provided originally by *The New York Times* editors, except when those referred to current events rather than the deal.

The dates on which the columns first appeared are shown. However, in a few cases obsolete material has been updated. Thus, for example, a column written in 1971 may include a reference to 1981.

The New York Times
♦ BRIDGE SERIES ♥
GRAND SLAMS

♠ ♣

CHAPTER 1
OPENING LEADS

It seems appropriate to lead off with leads. The first two examples suggest an exception to the conventional wisdom which calls for safe leads against grand slams. An attacking lead in dummy's long, strong suit can sometimes force the declarer to make a premature decision at the first trick. The remaining deals feature a small paradox and a couple of sad stories.

On Attack at the Cavendish

The basic guideline for leading against grand slams is to choose something safe. But there are rare occasions when this principle should be ignored, and the opening leader should select something unsafe—or apparently unsafe.

In the diagramed deal played at New York's famous Cavendish Club, North–South bid to a reasonable grand slam. North opened with a weak two-bid, and followed with a slightly eccentric rebid. The forcing response of two notrump asked him to describe his hand further, and the rebid of three notrump theoretically showed a solid diamond suit. North decided to regard the J–10 of diamonds as the equivalent of the queen, partly because a rebid of three diamonds would have sounded too discouraging.

South jumped confidently to seven notrump. Expecting to find a dummy with A K Q x x x in diamonds, he could count thirteen tricks if either minor suit came home. Even with the actual North hand, the grand slam was still an excellent bet.

On a neutral lead, South would have tested the clubs, and, if this suit proved unsatisfactory, he would have fallen back on diamonds, taking a first-round finesse against the queen.

Notice that the percentage play in diamonds is to finesse immediately. Playing a top honor first in case East has a singleton queen would be a bad error, for East is much more likely to have a small singleton than a singleton queen.

But this normal sequence of events, which would have succeeded, was disturbed by Gino Scalamandre, sitting West. Knowing that the diamonds were all on his left, he could tell that a diamond lead was safe. So he put the diamond eight on the table, hoping to confuse the issue for South or to force him to make a premature decision.

South could, of course, have made the contract by finessing immediately, but that would have been a foolish play, putting all his eggs in the diamond basket. Naturally and correctly, he won with the king in dummy and played the ace and king of clubs to test that suit. When this suit failed him he could fall back on diamonds, but there was no longer any way to make thirteen tricks.

The declarer spent a little time trying to guess whether West had led from Q x x in diamonds or x x x, the only combinations that could help. He eventually took the diamond finesse, which was right, up to a point.

But when East discarded, it was all over. South discarded his spade jack on the diamond winner and entered his hand with a major-suit lead. He surrendered a club to East for down one, and ruefully congratulated Scalamandre on his brilliant opening lead.

August 28, 1976

4

NORTH (D)
♠ 9 5 4
♡ 6 3
◇ A K J 10 7 4
♣ 10 7

WEST
♠ 10 8 7 3 2
♡ Q 10 2
◇ Q 8 5 2
♣ 3

EAST
♠ Q 6
♡ J 9 8 7 5 4
◇ 6
♣ J 8 6 5

SOUTH
♠ A K J
♡ A K
◇ 9 3
♣ A K Q 9 4 2

Neither side was vulnerable.
The bidding:

North	East	South	West
2 ◇	Pass	2 NT	Pass
3 NT	Pass	7 NT	Pass
Pass	Pass		

West led the diamond eight.

A Leading Role for Fred Karpin

Almost all players throughout the bridge world nowadays take for granted the 4-3-2-1 point-count for aces, kings, queens, and jacks, sometimes adding half a point for each ten. Those who have learned the game in the last quarter of a century tend to think, wrongly, that this is the only conceivable way to value bridge hands.

The idea goes back at least to 1915, when Bryant McCampbell of St. Louis recommended 4-3-2-1 for auction bridge. When contract bridge gained favor, this count was adopted by the Grand Old Man of Bridge, Milton C. Work. His name was attached to it, and he included it in the Official System in 1931. But like many other good ideas it was washed away by the fast-flowing Culbertson tide and for the next two decades American players zealously counted honor tricks, which were complex and not very accurate.

The point-count caught on in England and was in general use in the 1930s and 1940s. In a book entitled *Contract Simplicitas,* published in 1933, a British judge using the pseudonym "Criticus" recommended 4-3-2-1-½ together with a series of distributional adjustments that took into account extra trump length, long-side suits, and, varying with the degree of support, short suits in the responding hand when raising. Point-count was basic to the Acol System which began in the thirties and has been standard there ever since.

The tide turned in the United States in the late forties with the appearance of a booklet by Richard Miller and books by Fred Karpin and Charles Goren, in that order. They included distributional valuation in different ways. Karpin, the first to make a major impact in this direction, suggested extra points for long suits. Goren, adopting a Canadian proposal, advocated points for short suits. Players at all levels soon found that counting points, adjusting for distribution by points or by instinct, was much more accurate than honor tricks or other methods.

Karpin, a resident of Silver Spring, Maryland, has long been one of the country's most successful writers and teachers. On the diagramed deal, played long ago, he produced a brilliant inferential lead to defeat a grand slam. The clue was in the bidding, to which he listened with great care.

This was in the days before five-card major openings became popular, and North opened one heart prepared to bid diamonds at his next turn. South showed slam interest by jumping to three clubs. He followed with Blackwood, which, like point-count, had taken hold in the face of Culbertson's disapproval. When North showed two aces, South rightly tried for seven notrump. He felt sure of thirteen tricks if he could run clubs, and, if the club suit failed him, the notrump slam might still come home with tricks in the other suits. This calculation was accurate: Seven clubs would have been doomed by the trump split, but seven notrump was due to succeed against any normal lead.

NORTH (D)
♠ 3
♡ A J 10 9
◇ A Q J 10 2
♣ 8 6 4

WEST
♠ J 10 9 7
♡ 6 2
◇ K 9 8
♣ J 7 5 3

EAST
♠ 8 6 5 4 2
♡ 8 7 5 4 3
◇ 7 4 3
♣ —

SOUTH
♠ A K Q
♡ K Q
◇ 6 5
♣ A K Q 10 9 2

Both sides were vulnerable.
The bidding:

North	East	South	West
1 ♡	Pass	3 ♣	Pass
3 ◇	Pass	4 NT	Pass
5 ♡	Pass	7 NT	Pass
Pass	Pass		

West led the diamond nine.

Karpin as West knew that South must be relying on a long, strong club suit. And, unlike South, he knew that the clubs would not break. It was highly probable that the diamond ace was in the dummy, so he produced the diamond nine, putting South to the test immediately.

South would have needed x-ray vision to finesse. He put up the ace in dummy, and went down to unhappy defeat when the clubs failed to break. On a neutral lead, South would have tested clubs and then fallen back on diamonds. The finesse would have given him thirteen tricks without any need for the suit to break evenly.

March 30, 1980

A Most Ingenious Paradox

For the odd day in Leap Year an odd hand is perhaps appropriate. On the diagramed deal from the 1972 New York tournament some declarers in a grand slam contract received a helpful lead that took a finesse for them. They went down. Others received an unhelpful lead—and made the contract. W. S. Gilbert would no doubt have called this "a most ingenious paradox."

One of the successful declarers was the late Gene Neiger of New York, and the deal helped him to finish second in a Life Master Pair Championship with Joel Stuart of New York. Stuart's decision to open the bidding as North with a slightly eccentric Precision weak notrump, showing 13-15 points, instead of the orthodox systemic two-club bid, initiated a lengthy auction.

Two diamonds was "forcing Stayman," guaranteeing at least a game, and the next three bids were natural. Three spades was a waiting maneuver—South already knew his partner's distribution. With a minimum hand, North would have signed off in three notrump, so his next two bids were control-showing and indicated a willingness to cooperate in the move toward slam.

Four notrump was not Blackwood, but a natural request in the Italian style to show further assets, and five notrump showed that North was as suitable as he could possibly be for the purposes of a grand slam.

Against seven diamonds West made the unhelpful lead of a trump. South gave himself as many chances as possible by winning with the diamond jack in dummy and playing to ruff the third spade in dummy. He returned to his hand by cashing the heart ace and ruffing a heart. After drawing the missing trumps, he led to the club ace and ruffed another heart, giving himself the slight extra chance of the king falling.

When this failed, he eventually fell back on the club finesse and made the grand slam—because he had had an unhelpful lead. Declarers at other tables who received a helpful spade lead were less fortunate in the outcome.

The spade lead made it unnecessary to ruff a spade, so the right line of play was to draw trumps, cash the ace and king of clubs, and hope the queen falls doubleton. When this extra chance fails—a far better prospect than the heart king appearing in three rounds—South falls back on the heart finesse. And goes down.

Note that after the diamond lead, which necessitated a spade ruff, the declarer no longer had the entries to draw trumps, cash the ace-king of clubs, and then fall back on the heart finesse. He was forced into an inferior line of play, which happened to succeed.

February 29, 1972

8

NORTH (D)
♠ 10 5
♡ A Q 4 3
◊ J 2
♣ A K J 7 5

WEST
♠ 9 7 4 3
♡ J 6
◊ 9 7 4
♣ Q 9 8 2

EAST
♠ Q 8 6 2
♡ K 10 9 7 5 2
◊ 10 6
♣ 4

SOUTH
♠ A K J
♡ 8
◊ A K Q 8 5 3
♣ 10 6 3

Both sides were vulnerable.
The bidding:

North	East	South	West
1 NT	Pass	2 ◊	Pass
3 ♣	Pass	3 ◊	Pass
3 ♡	Pass	3 ♠	Pass
4 ♣	Pass	4 ◊	Pass
4 ♡	Pass	4 NT	Pass
5 NT	Pass	7 ◊	Pass
Pass	Pass		

West led the diamond four.

HAUNTED BY AN OLD DISASTER

One of the last links with the earliest years of the game is B. Jay Becker, a former world champion who won a national team championship in 1981 at the age of seventy-six. In his first year of competitive bridge, in 1932, he met with a disaster that has haunted him ever since. He held the East hand shown in the diagram in a rubber bridge game and after three passes made a sensible bid of six hearts.

He did not wish to allow his opponents into the bidding, and his chances of making twelve tricks were clearly good. Even today, with more sophisticated bidding methods available, most experts would choose the same bid.

Six hearts would have made easily, but unfortunately for Becker, South entered the proceedings with six spades. This unlikely development occurred because South had passed with a hand on which he should have opened four spades, or even one spade.

West persevered to seven hearts, perhaps feeling that his heart queen would be worth a trick. Seven hearts would have been doomed to a one-trick defeat, but the improbable contract of seven clubs would have succeeded if the opponents had obligingly led spades.

North, however, was happy to continue to seven spades. His hand was ideal for this contract, and he could not be certain that seven hearts would fail. East naturally doubled, somewhat upset at being deprived of the chance to play a heart slam.

An expert with the West cards would perhaps hit on the killing lead of a club, judging that a heart lead would be ruffed and that East must have a very strong side suit. But West made the routine lead of a heart, and South ruffed happily in the dummy.

In normal circumstances, South would expect to lose a diamond trick and a club trick, for down two. But South saw that the circumstances were not normal. East was marked by the bidding with at most one diamond, for he would not have risked a six-bid holding two quick losers in one suit.

South, therefore, entered his hand with a trump lead and led the diamond jack. This won the trick when West refused to cover, and it was then an easy matter to continue diamonds after drawing the remaining trump and discard the club loser on a diamond winner in the dummy.

When North–South had made the doubled grand slam, and the players had completed a difficult arithmetical calculation based on a scoring table that has since been revised, West apologized for not leading a club.

"Not at all," said Becker, gallantly shouldering the blame. "It was my fault. I should have passed the hand out!"

February 13, 1971

10

```
                    NORTH
                    ♠ J 9 6 3
                    ♡ —
                    ◇ A K 9 6 3
                    ♣ 8 6 4 2
WEST                                    EAST
♠ 10 7                                  ♠ —
♡ Q 9 3                                 ♡ A K J 10 8 6 5 2
◇ Q 8 7 2                               ◇ 10
♣ J 10 7 3                              ♣ A K Q 9
                    SOUTH (D)
                    ♠ A K Q 8 5 4 2
                    ♡ 7 4
                    ◇ J 5 4
                    ♣ 5
```

East and West were vulnerable.
The bidding:

South	West	North	East
Pass	Pass	Pass	6 ♡
6 ♠	7 ♡	7 ♠	Dbl.
Pass	Pass	Pass	

West led the heart three.

THREE ACES ARE NOT ENOUGH

People who speak similar languages, such as the Germans and Dutch, or the Spanish and Portuguese, often run into some confusion when they try to communicate with each other verbally. Such problems arise in speech and bridge where Americans and British are concerned.

A New York bridge player who visits a London club and takes part in a game must decide whether he will stick to his usual bidding style, hoping his partners will be familiar with Standard American, or attempt the English Acol style. North gambled on the second alternative on the diagramed deal, which was played at England's most famous fictional club, the Griffins. It was reported in *Bridge Magazine* by Victor Mollo, who is perhaps the world's most entertaining bridge writer.

The American visitor held the North cards, and his partner was the Rueful Rabbit, known equally for his enthusiasm, his incompetence, and his luck. North had wisely rejected the Rabbit's offer to play American methods, but his own knowledge was tested when his partner's one-heart bid was overcalled with one spade by a conservative West player.

The raise to four hearts would be normal in the United States as a preemptive action, indicating great distributional support for hearts but little high-card strength. In England, unfortunately, this jump to game implies a much better hand, and South set his sights on a slam. Being a Rabbit, he naturally dragged out his favorite weapon, the Blackwood convention, which should virtually never be used by a player who has a void suit.

If North had shown two aces, South would not have known whether to bid a slam. If one of North's aces was in clubs, a 50–50 chance, there would be two top losers in a slam. If not, there would only be one top loser.

If North had shown one ace, as he would normally do, South would have had to settle in five hearts, and be in some danger of losing three top tricks. Unfortunately for the partnership, North was guiltily aware that his four-heart bid was an exaggeration by English standards, and wanted to slow his partner down. He indulged in a white lie, bidding five clubs to deny an ace.

South had already made up his mind that his partner held two or three aces, and he could not credit the fact that his partner was aceless. He therefore concluded that his partner held all four aces, the alternative meaning of the five-club response to Blackwood. This was an implausible assumption, for North would have made a stronger bid over one spade with such a hand.

West was unable to believe his ears, and, when he doubled, South expressed his faith in his partner's bidding by redoubling. West led his singleton trump for safety's sake, and the awful truth was revealed to the declarer. He won in his hand with the king, and promptly led the dia-

```
                    NORTH
                    ♠ 9 5 4
                    ♡ A 8 7 6 5 3
                    ◇ 7
                    ♣ 9 8 7
WEST                                    EAST
♠ A Q 10 7 5                            ♠ J 3 2
♡ 9                                     ♡ 2
◇ A Q 3 2                               ◇ 6 5
♣ A Q J                                 ♣ K 10 6 5 4 3 2
                    SOUTH (D)
                    ♠ K 8
                    ♡ K Q J 10 4
                    ◇ K J 10 9 8 4
                    ♣ —
```

Both sides were vulnerable.
The bidding:

South	West	North	East
1 ♡	1 ♠	4 ♡	Pass
4 NT	Pass	5 ♣	Pass
7 ♡	Dbl.	Pass	Pass
Redbl.	Pass	Pass	Pass

West led the heart nine.

---

mond seven from dummy—from the wrong hand, of course. East alertly demanded that this misdemeanor be corrected, and South gloomily led the diamond four from his own hand.

West wanted his partner to have the lead in order to play a black suit so he played low. It took South some time to realize that dummy's seven had won the trick. When he did so, he returned to his hand with a trump lead and played a diamond. It was then an easy matter for South to ruff out West's ace and queen, and discard dummy's spades on his diamond winners.

West resented his partner's suggestion that he should not have doubled. "With three aces you wouldn't double a grand slam?"

"Not if I didn't intend to make at least one of them," snarled East.

South sat in a daze while North expressed his approval of the British bidding system: "I know of no other method by which we could have reached a grand slam with those cards," he said admiringly.

February 21, 1971

CHAPTER 2
PLANNING

This section describes four deals that severely tested dummy-play ability, and three of the four declarers passed the test. The first deal, as foreshadowed in the original text, received an international award: the Bols Brilliancy Prize for 1983. The fifth and final deal shows a little magic: a "sure" trump trick for a defender disappears.

A Prize-Winning Tour de Force

Some deals seem destined for recognition by those who award prizes, and the diagramed example from the 1983 Spingold Knockout Teams was spotted as a likely candidate immediately it was played. Eventually it received the 1983 Bols Brilliancy Prize awarded by the Dutch liqueur manufacturer.

Sitting South was Marv Rosenblatt of Hartford playing with Art Waldmann of Rocky Hill, Connecticut.

Playing against two former world champions, Paul Soloway and Bob Goldman, they followed the route shown to seven spades. After a slow start, South eventually located an ace in the North hand and invited the grand slam with a cue-bid of six diamonds.

North decided that his spade queen must be the card that was needed, as indeed it would have been if South had held 5-1-1-6 distribution.

South was hoping to find four trumps in dummy, which the three-spade raise had suggested. As it was, there were only twelve tricks in view even if the clubs could be run without loss. But Rosenblatt found a way to conjure up a thirteenth, which is not obvious even looking at the whole deal.

He won the heart king lead, and led the club ten to the ace, an important unblocking move. Then he cashed the spade ace and led to the queen.

He now had to hope that East had begun with exactly three spades and J x x x of clubs, not too unlikely since West's overcall had marked him with diamond length.

The club nine was finessed, and two more club winners provided diamond discards from dummy. That set up a diamond ruff in dummy to dispose of the loser in the closed hand, and a heart ruff allowed the last trump to be drawn.

Rosenblatt's tour de force earned his team 11 international match points, but, as it turned out, in a losing cause.

August 12, 1983

```
                    NORTH (D)
                    ♠ Q 5 3
                    ♡ A 9 7 6 2
                    ◊ 7 6 4
                    ♣ 10 3
WEST                                EAST
♠ 8 2                               ♠ J 9 4
♡ K Q J                             ♡ 10 8 4 3
◊ K 9 8 5 3 2                       ◊ Q 10
♣ 8 6                               ♣ J 7 4 2
                    SOUTH
                    ♠ A K 10 7 6
                    ♡ 5
                    ◊ A J
                    ♣ A K Q 9 5
```

East and West were vulnerable.
The bidding:

North	East	South	West
Pass	Pass	1 ♣	1 ◊
1 ♡	Pass	2 ♠	Pass
3 ♠	Pass	4 NT	Pass
5 ◊	Pass	6 ◊	Pass
7 ♠	Pass	Pass	Pass

West led the heart king.

A Clue from a Phantom Save

Perhaps the most dramatic deal of the 1976 World Team Championship in Monte Carlo occurred when the Brazilian star Gabriel Chagas helped his team to score a narrow victory over the United States by making a fascinating grand slam.

The bidding, as shown, began with diamonds being bid from the North side, following the Brazilian version of the Precision system. Two notrump simply showed a powerful hand, and three clubs was ambiguous, showing either a hand with one minor suit or a hand with both majors. South did not choose to find out and launched into Blackwood. When he finally bid seven diamonds, a contract that would probably have failed, Ira Rubin, the American West, decided to save in seven spades.

This could have been doubled and down eight tricks for a penalty of 1,500, but Chagas, as South, persevered to seven notrump. After West made the safe lead of a diamond, the declarer examined his prospects and had some reason to believe that the club finesse would fail, since spade length was on his left.

South ran six rounds of diamonds, cashed the spade ace, and played the last diamond, producing this position:

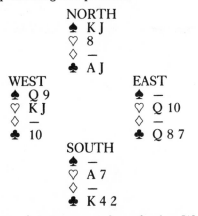

```
                      NORTH
                      ♠ K J
                      ♡ 8
                      ◇ —
                      ♣ A J
        WEST                      EAST
        ♠ Q 9                     ♠ —
        ♡ K J                     ♡ Q 10
        ◇ —                       ◇ —
        ♣ 10                      ♣ Q 8 7
                      SOUTH
                      ♠ —
                      ♡ A 7
                      ◇ —
                      ♣ K 4 2
```

The king and ace of clubs were taken, forcing West to part with a heart. The play of the spade king then ruined East, who was caught in the second stage of a nonsimultaneous double squeeze.

In the replay, the Americans rested in six diamonds, and Brazil gained 13 international match points. So Rubin had considerable cause to regret his save over seven diamonds, which gave the declarer a vital clue. If he had passed the U.S.A. would almost certainly have won the match and improved its score by 5 Victory Points.

May 5, 1976

NORTH
- ♠ K J 10
- ♡ 8 6 2
- ◇ K 3
- ♣ A J 9 6 5

WEST (D)
- ♠ Q 9 8 7 6 5
- ♡ K J 4
- ◇ J 7
- ♣ 10 3

EAST
- ♠ 4 3 2
- ♡ Q 10 9 5 3
- ◇ 8 6
- ♣ Q 8 7

SOUTH
- ♠ A
- ♡ A 7
- ◇ A Q 10 9 5 4 2
- ♣ K 4 2

North and South were vulnerable.
The bidding:

West	North	East	South
Pass	1 ◇	Pass	2 NT
Pass	3 ♣	Pass	4 NT
Pass	5 ◇	Pass	5 NT
Pass	6 ♡	Pass	7 ◇
7 ♠	Pass	Pass	7 NT
Pass	Pass	Pass	

West led the diamond jack.

GIVING THE GAME AWAY IN A SLAM

Several excellent books have been written on the subject of card-reading, but one of them has a good claim to be considered the best of the bunch. It is *How to Read Your Opponent's Cards* by Mike Lawrence, published in 1973 by Prentice-Hall.

The author is a young, taciturn Californian who won two world titles as a member of the Aces team before he resigned from that prestigious group. His purpose is expressed by his subtitle: "The Bridge Experts' Way to Locate Missing High Cards."

There is no mention of coups, squeezes, or other advanced plays. Instead, the reader is taught how to guess which opponent has a vital ace, king, or queen.

Lawrence begins with some simple examples on which players of some experience would go astray, and then ranges through negative inferences and assumptions to insubstantial psychological clues.

The need to modify one's planning when additional information indicates that the original plan will fail is illustrated by the diagramed deal, one of the most difficult in the book. The hero was another member of the Aces team, Bob Hamman, who found himself in seven clubs in a rubber bridge game. The contract was a reasonable one, but, nevertheless, North's bidding was overoptimistic. If Hamman had held two spades instead of one, the contract would have been entirely hopeless.

As it was, Hamman had two chances of avoiding a heart loser. If the spades split four–three, he could establish the fifth spade to discard a heart from the closed hand. And if this failed, he could fall back on a diamond finesse to dispose of dummy's loser.

West led the heart nine, and East signaled loudly but indiscreetly with the king when the ace was played from dummy. South now knew that East had begun with king-queen-ten of hearts and probably the jack as well. The ten would have been less revealing.

The spade ace was cashed at the second trick and a spade was ruffed. A trump lead to dummy and another spade ruff revealed the bad news—the fifth spade in dummy could not be established. The time had come to assess all the available information before resorting to the diamond finesse.

South knew all about the black suits, quite a lot about the heart suit, but nothing about the diamond suit. East had begun with K J 10 9 8 of spades, a singleton club, and very probably K Q J 10 of hearts. If he had the diamond king to boot he would have opened the bidding.

So Hamman decided that West held the diamond king, and considered whether to ruff two diamonds in the hope of establishing the queen. If West held three diamonds, this could be done. But if West held three diamonds, his distribution would be 2-7-3-1. A seven-card heart suit was

```
                    NORTH
                    ♠ A 7 6 5 4
                    ♡ A 4
                    ◇ 3
                    ♣ K Q 9 8 5
WEST                                    EAST (D)
♠ Q 2                                   ♠ K J 10 9 8
♡ 9 8 7 5 2                             ♡ K Q J 10
◇ K 9 6 5 2                             ◇ J 8 7
♣ 3                                     ♣ 2
                    SOUTH
                    ♠ 3
                    ♡ 6 3
                    ◇ A Q 10 4
                    ♣ A J 10 7 6 4
```

Both sides were vulnerable.
The bidding:

East	South	West	North
Pass	1 ♣	Pass	1 ♠
Pass	2 ♣	Pass	4 NT
Pass	5 ♡	Pass	7 ♣
Pass	Pass	Pass	

West led the heart nine.

hardly possible. It would have meant that West had led the heart nine from J 10 9 8 7 5 2. So South ruled out that possibility.

There was only one chance consistent with the evidence available. South had to hope that East held the diamond jack, guarded not more than twice.

So South cashed the diamond ace, ruffed a diamond, and ruffed a spade. Next he led the diamond queen according to plan, and West covered with the king. Dummy ruffed, and when East produced the jack it was all over. The diamond ten was established to take care of the heart loser in dummy.

"That was a wonderful bid, partner," Hamman declared, with his tongue firmly in his cheek. "How did you know I had the ten of diamonds?"

November 8, 1973

ENTRY SHORTAGE WITH FIVE QUICK TRICKS

If more than one eight-card trump fit is available for slam purposes, the solidity of the suit is often the crucial factor. This was the case in the diagramed deal, reported from a rubber bridge game by Lee Hazen of New York, counsel to the American Contract Bridge League and a world championship contender in 1956.

The opening bid of two clubs was strong and artificial, and North made a waiting response of two diamonds rather than show his length and strength immediately with three diamonds. Both players bid their long suits, and North made another rather odd decision by showing his weak four-card club suit.

This was music to South's ears, and he alarmed his partner by jumping to a grand slam. Furthermore, because of the opening bid, South became the declarer and North had to suffer as dummy, wondering whether he had contributed to an overoptimistic contract.

After an opening heart lead, South needed to do some careful planning. He must assume that the trumps will split three–two, and he must try to develop spades: Diamonds cannot be used because it would be necessary to ruff with a high trump, thereby losing a trump trick.

If both black suits split normally, it will be easy to make thirteen tricks. So South should look for some way to guard against a four–one spade split. This can be done if one defender has exactly four spades and three trumps, which happens to be the situation.

It might appear that South has a sufficiency of entries, but, in fact, he has barely enough, and he must not waste them. He should win the opening heart lead in dummy, draw two rounds of trumps, and begin spades, ruffing the second round in dummy. If both opponents follow twice, all is well and he can simply draw the last trump.

As it happens, however, West is unable to ruff in. So South can return to the heart ace, ruff another spade, and ruff a diamond. He draws the missing trump and scores the rest of his spades without even needing the A–K of diamonds in the dummy.

In practice, however, South failed to realize that he would need entries in his hand. He won the first trick with the heart ace and the grand slam became unmakable. When he had gone down he complained about North's four-club bid, but North had the last word. "If you cannot play them right," he retorted, "you shouldn't bid so much."

November 8, 1980

NORTH
- ♠ 5
- ♡ K 4
- ◇ A K 8 7 4 2
- ♣ 6 5 4 3

WEST
- ♠ 6
- ♡ Q 10 8 7 3 2
- ◇ J 9 6 5
- ♣ 10 8

EAST
- ♠ Q J 9 7
- ♡ J 9 5
- ◇ Q 10 3
- ♣ J 9 2

SOUTH (D)
- ♠ A K 10 8 4 3 2
- ♡ A 6
- ◇ —
- ♣ A K Q 7

Both sides were vulnerable.
The bidding:

South	West	North	East
2 ♣	Pass	2 ◇	Pass
2 ♠	Pass	3 ◇	Pass
3 ♠	Pass	4 ♣	Pass
7 ♣	Pass	Pass	Pass

West led the heart seven.

THE DISAPPEARING TRUMP TRICK

Miraculous escapes and disappearances have always been a subject of absorbing interest to bridge theorists as well as to stage magicians. When sure trump tricks vanish away, there is always a story.

Some positions are relatively well known, such as the situation in which one defender has a doubleton queen and his partner a tripleton jack. Much more unusual is this trump suit:

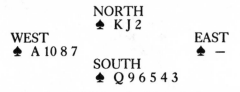

If South can ruff twice in his hand without being overruffed he can then lead toward the dummy. West must duck, and if South can then ruff something with his queen at the eleventh trick, West can only score one trick.

This was described recently by the British expert Martin Hoffman in a brilliant book entitled *More Tales of Hoffman*. He followed with an even more remarkable example, reported to him by Giorgio Belladonna of Italy, the world's top-ranked player, and shown in the diagram.

North and South have overbid to seven spades by a route that is not on record. In the hypothetical auction shown, North is to blame for using Blackwood and leaving himself a guess at the finish. If he feels bullish about grand slam prospects, he should bid five notrump, the grand slam force, at his second turn.

It has always been assumed that a declarer with such a trump holding must lose at least one trick. So the grand slam is hopeless. Or is it?

With the distribution as shown South can survive. He should win in dummy, ruff a diamond, and use heart entries to ruff two more diamonds. Then he can lead to the club ace, ruff a heart, and cash two more clubs to reach the position in the facing subdiagram.

NORTH
- ♠ Q 2
- ♡ A K 10 8 7
- ◇ A 6 5 3
- ♣ A 4

WEST
- ♠ 10 8 7
- ♡ J 5 4
- ◇ Q J 10 8
- ♣ 9 7 5

EAST
- ♠ K 9
- ♡ Q 6 2
- ◇ K 9 7 2
- ♣ 8 6 3 2

SOUTH (D)
- ♠ A J 6 5 4 3
- ♡ 9 3
- ◇ 4
- ♣ K Q J 10

Both sides were vulnerable.
The bidding:

South	West	North	East
1 ♠	Pass	2 ♡	Pass
2 ♠	Pass	4 NT	Pass
5 ◇	Pass	5 NT	Pass
6 ◇	Pass	7 ♠	Pass
Pass	Pass		

West led the diamond queen.

NORTH
- ♠ Q 2
- ♡ 10
- ◇ —
- ♣ —

WEST
- ♠ 10 8 7
- ♡ —
- ◇ —
- ♣ —

EAST
- ♠ K 9
- ♡ —
- ◇ —
- ♣ 8

SOUTH
- ♠ A J
- ♡ —
- ◇ —
- ♣ J

When the club jack is led, the defense is helpless. And an original trump lead does not defeat the grand slam. The ending shown works if the spade seven, two, nine, and jack have already been played.

September 16, 1984

CHAPTER 3
FINESSING

It is true, but only just true, to say that a grand slam that needs a winning finesse should not be bid. But if you think that the grand needs a finesse at worst you should bid it: If you fail to bid a lay-down grand, you have made a major error, but if you reach one that needs a finesse, you have made a minor one. These deals concern tricks, percentages, antipercentages, and some more bizarre aspects of finessing.

PSYCHOLOGICAL FINESSE

A two-way finesse is never a guess. That statement, like virtually all other sweeping generalizations about bridge, is untrue. But it is not far from the truth, and the substitution of "hardly ever" for "never" would give it validity.

This assumes that the two-way finesse is for a queen. (A two-way finesse for a jack, a rarer bird, is quite often a complete guess.) There are some highly improper but interesting ways to improve one's prospects, all based on provoking a reaction from the opponent holding the queen. You can, like P. Hal Sims, think a long time in the hope that the player with the queen will attempt to show nonchalance by making a remark, lighting a cigarette, or ordering a drink. If this fails, you can then lead rapidly from the wrong hand and see who objects. And at rubber bridge with one trump honor in dummy, you can make a premature and mendacious claim of 100 honors in the hope that someone will object.

Consider this layout:

NORTH
♣ A J 10 5

SOUTH
♣ K 9 8 2

If this is a side suit and South's holding has not been shown in the auction, it is right to lead the nine at an early stage. A good player in the West position may cover with the queen, fearing that you have a doubleton nine.

In most cases, however, percentages must be considered. If one opponent is known to have length in another suit, he is less likely to have the crucial queen. And the high-card points in the defenders' hands may offer a clue and so may the absence of an opening lead in the key suit.

If the nine is missing, there is usually a clear-cut way to play. With the heart suit shown in the diagram, for example, one should normally play West for the queen, taking a first-round finesse. This gains when East has a small singleton and loses to a singleton queen. It appears to lose also when West has a singleton nine, but South has a chance to change course.

When this deal was played in a duplicate game, it might seem that almost any four-one trump split was due to wreck South's optimistic grand slam. But Barry Schwartz of the psychology department at Swarthmore College struggled home with thirteen tricks by assuming a favorable distribution in the other suits.

The bidding calls for some explanation. Two clubs was strong and artificial, and the response of two hearts showed, by partnership agree-

```
                    NORTH (D)
                    ♠ A K J 10 9 8
                    ♡ A J 10
                    ◇ A K 8
                    ♣ A
WEST                                    EAST
♠ Q 5 4 2                               ♠ 7 3
♡ Q 9 6 2                               ♡ 3
◇ 10 7 4                                ◇ J 9 5 2
♣ 8 6                                   ♣ Q 10 9 5 3 2
                    SOUTH
                    ♠ 6
                    ♡ K 8 7 5 4
                    ◇ Q 6 3
                    ♣ K J 7 4
```

Both sides were vulnerable.
The bidding:

North	West	South	East
2 ♣	Pass	2 ♡	Pass
2 ♠	Pass	3 ♡	Pass
3 ♠	Pass	3 NT	Pass
4 ◇	Pass	4 ♡	Pass
7 ♡	Pass	Pass	Pass

West led the club eight.

ment, two kings or an ace. North now knew that the partnership held all the aces and kings; so he was thinking in grand slam terms.

North might have bid five notrump after three hearts, requiring a grand slam, if South held the heart queen as well as the king. But there were chances of making seven spades or seven notrump even if the heart queen was missing.

North bid seven hearts in the expectation that his partner held either the heart queen or a six-card suit. As it was, the declarer had a lot of work to do. He won the club lead in dummy, cashed the spade ace, and ruffed a spade. He finessed the heart ten successfully, crossed to the diamond queen, and repeated the trump finesse.

East's discard of a club was a blow, but Schwartz saw that he still had a chance. He needed to find West with 4-4-3-2 distribution, in that order, which would permit all the side-suit winners to be cashed safely. He cashed the spade king and ruffed another spade. He cashed the club king and two more diamond winners.

All this passed off peacefully, and West was reduced to the queen-nine of trumps. But South still had the ace and king, and crossruffed the last two tricks to make his grand slam.

February 7, 1982

SWINGING AGAINST THE ODDS

One of the main objectives of any bridge tournament is to minimize luck and maximize skill. Luck cannot be eliminated completely, except perhaps in a par contest in which prearranged deals set specific problems to the contestants, but its impact can be reduced by the method of scoring employed.

A game contract or a slam contract that has about an even chance of success automatically introduces a substantial luck factor. One pair will gain while another loses, and nobody has done anything to deserve either.

It is this type of situation that has led to the progressive abandonment of total-point scoring:

Tobias Stone was North and Alvin Roth was South, and the slightly surprising original pass by North was in accordance with their system, which prescribes high standards for opening bids. Four clubs and five clubs were Gerber bids asking for aces and kings, and North reached for the grand slam when he found that the partnership held all the aces and kings.

West led a club, which seemed least likely to hurt the defense, and Roth had to guess the heart situation. He played off all his winners in the black suits and East had to discard a heart in order to keep his diamond guard.

After making diamond winners and the heart ace, Roth led the heart jack toward dummy and finessed, going down two. He knew that West had started with four hearts and East with three, so the odds slightly favored finding the queen in the West hand.

When the hand was replayed, Pedro Cabral, Greenwich, Connecticut, played in seven spades from the North position, a very slightly superior contract. He also discovered the heart split by careful counting, and played East for the queen of hearts.

Cabral knew that this was a slightly inferior play, but also knew that his team needed an enormous gain to win the match. He realized that if the opposing team played the hand correctly and he did the same, the match would be lost.

Bowing acknowledgment to the helpful heart queen, the Cabral team, captained by Mrs. Sally Johnson, Westport, Connecticut, gained 2,510 total points and won the match by 180. This was a crucial match in the 1957 Spingold Trophy, and it was the last time that total points were used in a major national team championship.

June 14, 1964

```
                    NORTH (D)
                    ♠ A Q J 10 8
                    ♡ K 8 6
                    ◇ 6 5
                    ♣ Q J 10
WEST                                    EAST
♠ 6 4                                   ♠ 9 5 2
♡ 9 7 4 3                               ♡ Q 5 2
◇ 4                                     ◇ Q J 9 8 7 2
♣ 9 8 6 5 4 3                           ♣ 7
                    SOUTH
                    ♠ K 7 3
                    ♡ A J 10
                    ◇ A K 10 3
                    ♣ A K 2
```

Both sides were vulnerable.
The bidding:

North	East	South	West
Pass	Pass	2 NT	Pass
4 ♣	Pass	4 NT	Pass
5 ♣	Pass	5 NT	Pass
7 NT	Pass	Pass	Pass

CHINESE FINESSE

There are several oddities about a Chinese finesse. It is not a finesse, it is not Chinese, and Deng Xiaoping, Peking's senior Deputy Prime Minister and the best-known Chinese bridge player, has probably never heard of it.

If you lead an unsupported queen toward an ace in the dummy, the queen cannot, in theory, win the trick. But in practice, it will do so occasionally, because your left-hand opponent withholds his king in the belief that you have the jack.

In this crude form, the Chinese finesse rarely succeeds. But when smaller cards are involved, a shrewd declarer can sometimes take advantage of an unwary defender.

In the diagramed example, played at a 1979 Nassau-Suffolk double knockout team championship, the hero was eighteen-year-old Alex Pollenz of East Meadow, Long Island, who seems marked for future stardom. He and his teammates, Mitchell Pollenz, Ethan Stein, Mel Colchamiro, and Richard Sands, were the last undefeated team in the event, after scoring a 23-international-match-point victory over one of the country's strongest teams: Dave Berkowitz, Harold Lilie, Alan Sontag, and Peter Weichsel.

South opened the bidding with one heart, feeling that his distributional strength was sufficient compensation for his high-card weakness. And his subsequent bidding was equally aggressive.

The two notrump response, by partnership agreement, showed a hand worth a forcing raise in hearts. South had an ideal hand for Blackwood and jumped confidently to four notrump. The chance that North held only one ace was very slight in view of the failure of East–West to enter the auction.

A five-club response to Blackwood almost always shows a lack of aces. But it can also mean a complete collection and did so here.

South read this correctly and jumped to seven hearts: There was virtually no way North could have a forcing raise in hearts lacking all the aces and the cards South could see in his hand.

Seven hearts is an excellent contract, but it was unmakable as the card lay. With or without an opening club lead South is due to be defeated by the bad club break.

East attempted to indicate his desire for a ruff by doubling seven hearts. This was a Lightner double, and West should have worked out that a club lead was called for. He did not understand the message, but South did. He won the diamond lead in dummy, drew trumps ending in his hand, and led the club eight.

When West routinely played low, South played low from the dummy, bringing off an unusual version of the Chinese finesse. He was then able to continue clubs and eventually ruff out the club queen to make the doubled grand slam.

```
                    NORTH
                    ♠ A 6 5 4
                    ♡ A 10 4 3
                    ◇ A 8 5
                    ♣ A 4
WEST                                    EAST
♠ K J 8 3                               ♠ Q 10 9 2
♡ 6                                     ♡ J 9 5
◇ K 9 2                                 ◇ Q J 10 7 6 3
♣ Q 9 7 5 3                             ♣ —
                    SOUTH (D)
                    ♠ 7
                    ♡ K Q 8 7 2
                    ◇ 6
                    ♣ K J 10 8 6 2
```

Both sides were vulnerable.
The bidding:

South	West	North	East
1 ♡	Pass	2 NT	Pass
4 NT	Pass	5 ♣	Pass
7 ♡	Pass	Pass	Dbl.
Pass	Pass	Pass	

West led the diamond two.

Notice the crucial importance of the club seven. If South had held that card, his play of the eight would have been decisive. As it was, West could and should have played the nine on the eight, but he was not expecting his teenage opponent to take a Chinese finesse.

May 10, 1979

BEWARE OF FREE OFFERS

Something free is usually right but sometimes wrong. If it is fresh air, fresh water, or a concert in the park, by all means grab it. But if it is a free offer in the mail, a careful study of the fine print is recommended.

Much the same is true in bridge. If you are void in the suit led and dummy has the A–Q, you should usually, but not always, take the free finesse by playing the queen.

There may be rather more sophisticated reasons for refusing to take a free finesse. On the diagramed deal, Peter Weichsel, who has won several national titles and one world team championship, was looking well ahead.

Seven diamonds is an excellent contract. The final bid was slightly risky, for South could not be sure that his partner held the heart ace. But if that card was missing, the suit might not be led.

After a spade lead, South could have taken a free finesse of the jack, hoping that the queen was on his left, or a free finesse of the nine, hoping that the ten was on his left. But Weichsel visualized the distribution shown in the diagram, with both minor suits breaking badly, and refused both free finesses. He put up the spade king, led to the club ace, and ruffed a club.

He led a trump to his hand, and all would have been plain sailing if both defenders had followed. He would have been able to ruff another club loser with the diamond queen. He could no longer afford this, but he had another string to his bow. He led to the diamond queen, cashed the spade ace, and ruffed a spade. West's remaining trumps were drawn to produce this tricky position:

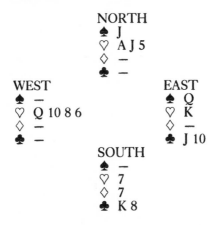

```
                    NORTH
                    ♠ J
                    ♡ A J 5
                    ◇ —
                    ♣ —
    WEST                        EAST
    ♠ —                         ♠ Q
    ♡ Q 10 8 6                  ♡ K
    ◇ —                         ◇ —
    ♣ —                         ♣ J 10
                    SOUTH
                    ♠ —
                    ♡ 7
                    ◇ 7
                    ♣ K 8
```

The stage was now set for one of the rarest endings in the game: a guard squeeze. When the last trump was led, a heart was thrown from

```
                    NORTH (D)
                    ♠ A K J 9
                    ♡ A J 5 4 2
                    ◇ Q 6 2
                    ♣ 7
WEST                                     EAST
♠ 6 5 2                                  ♠ Q 10 8 7 4 3
♡ Q 10 8 6                               ♡ K 9
◇ 10 9 8 3                               ◇ —
♣ Q 6                                    ♣ J 10 9 5 3
                    SOUTH
                    ♠ —
                    ♡ 7 3
                    ◇ A K J 7 5 4
                    ♣ A K 8 4 2
```

Both sides were vulnerable.
The bidding:

North	East	South	West
1 ♡	Pass	2 ◇	Pass
2 ♠	Pass	3 ♣	Pass
3 ◇	Pass	4 ♣	Pass
4 ◇	Pass	7 ◇	Pass
Pass	Pass		

West led the spade six.

the dummy. East could not spare a black card, and reluctantly gave up his heart king.

Now Weichsel cashed the club king, throwing dummy's spade loser, and took a heart finesse to bring home the grand slam.

Notice that this ending would have been unavailable if Weichsel had taken a free finesse at the first trick. He would then have had to destroy dummy's remaining spade loser in order to return to his hand after scoring the diamond queen.

November 13, 1980

THE MADMAN'S COUP

Some defensive plays are so ridiculous, so patently absurd, that a partner will immediately conclude that the player has lost his wits completely, or, more charitably, has pulled out the wrong card. Suppose that late in the play the remaining clubs lie like this:

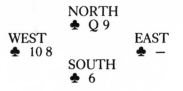

```
              NORTH
              ♣ Q 9
    WEST              EAST
    ♣ 10 8           ♣ —
              SOUTH
              ♣ 6
```

When South leads the six, West plays the eight, and South must guess whether to finesse or not. Only a madman in the West position would play the ten, making it unnecessary for South to guess. But in very special circumstances such a play might be right: He might be suffering, like Hamlet, from a "crafty madness."

Consider the diagramed deal from a 1972 Regional Open Pair Championship in Syracuse, New York. East's pre-emptive action after North opened with a strong, artificial two-club bid was actually rather mild; he might well have jumped to four hearts or even five in a bolder attempt to crowd the auction. Five hearts doubled would have failed by five tricks, but the 1,400 would be slightly less—significantly less at match points—than the vulnerable notrump slam actually available to North–South.

South's bid of four diamonds—three notrump would perhaps have been better—set a problem for North. He could have raised diamonds to five or six, but he chose a cue-bid of four hearts. South then used Blackwood, and North's response of five clubs clearly indicated four aces rather than none. When South discovered that his partner also held the diamond king he gambled on seven notrump.

West led his lone heart, and South won in dummy with the ace. He cashed the spade ace, the club ace, the spade king, and the club king. The appearance of the club jack from East made it likely, but not certain,

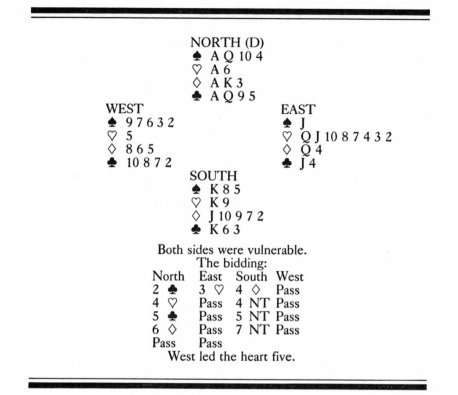

NORTH (D)
♠ A Q 10 4
♡ A 6
◇ A K 3
♣ A Q 9 5

WEST
♠ 9 7 6 3 2
♡ 5
◇ 8 6 5
♣ 10 8 7 2

EAST
♠ J
♡ Q J 10 8 7 4 3 2
◇ Q 4
♣ J 4

SOUTH
♠ K 8 5
♡ K 9
◇ J 10 9 7 2
♣ K 6 3

Both sides were vulnerable.
The bidding:

North	East	South	West
2 ♣	3 ♡	4 ◇	Pass
4 ♡	Pass	4 NT	Pass
5 ♣	Pass	5 NT	Pass
6 ◇	Pass	7 NT	Pass
Pass	Pass		

West led the heart five.

that a finesse against West in that suit would produce a fourth club trick. The position was now this:

NORTH
♠ Q 10
♡ 6
◇ A K 3
♣ Q 9

WEST
♠ 9 7 6
♡ —
◇ 8 6 5
♣ 10 8

EAST
♠ —
♡ Q J 10 7 4 3
◇ Q 4
♣ —

SOUTH
♠ 8
♡ K
◇ J 10 9 7 2
♣ 6

West was Chuck Lamprey of White Plains, New York, one of the country's finest young players. When South continued by leading the club six he routinely played low—and realized a fraction of a second too late that he had missed the chance of a lifetime to bring off the Madman's Coup, an entirely new maneuver in the literature of the game.

As Lamprey feared, South proceeded to misjudge the club situation. The declarer did not feel inclined to risk immediate defeat in his grand slam, so he played the club queen from dummy, disregarding the percentages. When the ten did not fall, he found himself forced into an antipercentage play in diamonds.

To make the rest of the tricks at this point, South had to make four diamond tricks. The normal play of entering the closed hand with a heart to take a diamond finesse was hopeless: West would simply refuse to cover the jack with the queen, and the suit would be blocked. The declarer would end up stranded in the dummy with the club nine as an unavoidable loser.

Seeing there was no help for it, South shrugged his shoulders and called for the ace and king of diamonds from the dummy. When the queen came tumbling from East, he put his cards on the table, proudly claiming the grand slam.

Now consider what would have happened if West had put up the club ten in the diagramed position, a spectacular lunacy. South would have had twelve sure tricks, and would simply need one extra diamond trick. He would postpone the diamond play until the twelfth trick, by cashing his black-suit winners, the diamond ace, and the heart king before leading the diamond jack.

At this point South would know that West held two diamonds to East's one. The odds would be three to two in favor of finessing, for the original three–two division of the suit would be the vital factor. So South would finesse and go down, a victim of the Madman's Coup.

December 24, 1972

CHAPTER 4

DECEPTIONS

Deceptions can be contrived in bidding, play, and defense. Two deals in this section, both from France, are moves by a defender and a declarer. We have a curious problem concerned with salvaging match points. And there are two remarkable doubles. One of these, in "Lightner is Darkener," would get my vote for the most imaginative call I have ever seen.

NEVER SAY ALWAYS

If you make an asinine play your opponent will sometimes start worrying about gift horses. In fact, an expert can, on occasion, make a defensive move that seems to have nothing to gain and everything to lose—and profit by the resulting confusion.

One would suppose that a player with a queen–ten combination in a suit, and no other cards in that suit, should always cover if an opponent leads the jack. But "always" is a dangerous word in bridge discussions, and the diagramed deal represents a remarkable example.

The deal was played in an international tournament in Cannes in the sixties. It was reported by Dr. Pierre Jais, one of the world's great players; the hero, sitting West, was Gerard Desrousseaux, a star of almost equal magnitude.

The strange bidding shown in the diagram illustrates a convention that is popular with many French experts. The responses to a strong artificial opening two-club bid show whether responder has any aces. Two diamonds would be negative, and suit bids from two hearts through three diamonds show the ace of the bid suit. Higher responses at the three-level show two aces in a special way: North's bid of three hearts, for example, showed two aces not of the same color and not of the same rank.

As it happens, all South needed to know was that his partner held two aces. But, if South's holding had been the spade ace and a void in diamonds, he would have known that North held the right aces to make a grand slam possible.

After both players had shown their long suits, South used a form of Blackwood. Since North had already revealed his aces, four notrump asked for kings and South was not surprised to receive a negative reply. Five notrump asked for queens, and if North had been able to indicate one queen, a grand slam in notrump would have been easy to bid and make.

As it was, South could only be sure of twelve tricks, but he reasoned that in seven spades he would at worst need to develop dummy's hearts with a ruff, and the club ace would be available as an entry eventually.

Against seven spades, West led the diamond queen and South won with the ace. He drew trumps, led the heart king, and followed with the jack. His plan was to try for a three–three division.

But instead of making the automatic play of covering the jack with the queen, Desrousseaux made the unconventional play of the ten. He was certain that South held only a doubleton heart, and also certain that South planned to play the ace from dummy.

West's certainty about the number of hearts originally held by South derived from a bidding clue, a play clue, and a defense clue. It was unlikely that South would have bid seven spades with a heart holding of

```
                    NORTH
                    ♠ 6 3
                    ♡ A 9 8 4 2
                    ◇ 7 6 4
                    ♣ A 6 2
WEST                                    EAST
♠ 5 2                                   ♠ 9 8 4
♡ Q 10 5                                ♡ 7 6 3
◇ Q J 10                                ◇ 9 8 5 3
♣ Q 10 5 4 3                            ♣ J 9 7
                    SOUTH (D)
                    ♠ A K Q J 10 7
                    ♡ K J
                    ◇ A K 2
                    ♣ K 8
```

Both sides were vulnerable.
The bidding:

South	West	North	East
2 ♣	Pass	3 ♡	Pass
3 ♠	Pass	4 ♡	Pass
4 NT	Pass	5 ♣	Pass
5 NT	Pass	6 ♣	Pass
7 ♠	Pass	Pass	Pass

West led the diamond queen.

K J x because South knew the queen was missing. Also, with a three-card holding, South would not have played the king and jack, an inconceivable play. And if East had begun with a doubleton, he would have begun a high-low signal when South led the king.

West's play of the ten naturally convinced South that East held the queen. So he put up the ace in dummy and played the nine, trying for a ruffing finesse against East.

When East played the seven on the nine, South confidently discarded his losing diamond. He was shaken when West produced the heart queen to beat the slam.

"Well defended, partner," said East, quite rightly.

"I couldn't have gone wrong if I had been missing the heart nine or eight," observed South sadly.

"Timeo Gallos et dona ferentes," muttered North, who was something of a Latin scholar, and knew all about opponents bearing gifts.

August 1, 1971

LIGHTNER IS DARKENER

One of the most imaginative bidding actions in the history of the game was produced on the diagramed deal by a New York expert who has never been lacking in imagination. It occurred during the first round of the 1983 Reisinger Knockout Teams, the prestige event of New York's traditional Eastern Regionals, and the player in the West seat was John Lowenthal.

It was no surprise to Lowenthal that his opponents were able to bid a slam, but it was a shock to find them at the seven-level before he had a chance to pass: An opening three-club bid had been raised to a grand slam after East had bid hearts.

Lowenthal does not like to pass, and, after a little thought, he came forth with a double. It might seem that he had no hope of defeating the contract, and indeed he had not. But he had worked out the likely layout of the cards around the table and had a very subtle thought.

To justify his bid, South must have some good club support, presumably three cards, and all the other suits controlled. Somebody had to have spades, and there was good reason to think that South held length and strength, offering the prospect of discards. And it was highly probable that North–South held ten clubs between them, leaving East with a void.

When the double came around to South, he thought what Lowenthal hoped he would think. The double was a Lightner action, asking for an unusual lead. West must be void in spades, and was trying to encourage his partner to find a lead in that suit for the decisive ruff.

Not knowing that West had come up with a psychic Lightner double, South beat a retreat, not unnaturally, to seven spades. Lowenthal doubled again, putting great faith in his analysis of the situation. He then led a club.

South was a large, aggressive character. He put his cards face upward on the table and glared at East. Snarling, he said, "If you are going to ruff this, I'm going to kick you . . ."

East was small and nervous, with a strong sense of self-preservation. He produced a trump to beat the slam, got up from the table, and set off at a great rate for the horizon.

November 4, 1983

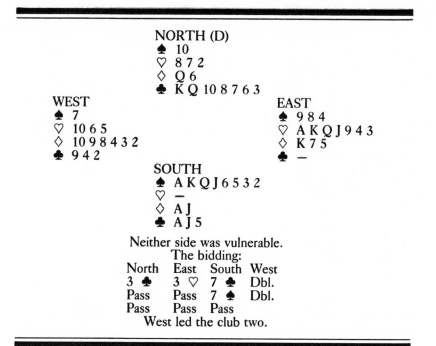

NORTH (D)
♠ 10
♡ 8 7 2
◇ Q 6
♣ K Q 10 8 7 6 3

WEST
♠ 7
♡ 10 6 5
◇ 10 9 8 4 3 2
♣ 9 4 2

EAST
♠ 9 8 4
♡ A K Q J 9 4 3
◇ K 7 5
♣ —

SOUTH
♠ A K Q J 6 5 3 2
♡ —
◇ A J
♣ A J 5

Neither side was vulnerable.
The bidding:

North	East	South	West
3 ♣	3 ♡	7 ♣	Dbl.
Pass	Pass	7 ♠	Dbl.
Pass	Pass	Pass	

West led the club two.

HIGH BID CALLS FOR LOW PLAY

Many players shy away from tournaments because they "don't understand all those new-fangled conventions." But it is a reason that does not hold water.

At all levels of tournament play except the very highest, a player is unlikely to meet an unfamiliar convention more than once or twice in a session. When he does, the convention will be explained to him, via the "alert" procedure, and the chance that he will be at a disadvantage is very small. And many major tournaments have events in which conventions are restricted.

The inexperienced tournament player does suffer from a quite different disadvantage, however: He and his partner are likely to be less skilled in natural bidding. Most of their opponents will have discussed a variety of situations in advance and will know, for example, whether a bid is forcing, invitational, or weak. They will also know what point-range it implies and whether it indicates any particular suit-length.

All this is not a matter of artificial convention but of natural understanding. The more practiced the partnership, the more such understandings they will have. For example, most experts will know the meaning of a raise from one notrump to five notrump. To the lesser ranks it is likely to be a mystery.

The diagramed example occurred in a book that may well prove to be the outstanding contribution of 1984 to the literature of the game. It is *Play Bridge with Mike Lawrence,* and the eponymous author, a former world champion, was sitting South in a pair event.

North, a somewhat less experienced player, had a hand on which he should have bid a direct six notrump. Instead, for no good reason, he bid five notrump.

South knew the expert meaning of the bid: an invitation to bid a grand slam. Concluding, wrongly, that his partner was equally educated, he bid the grand slam. Perhaps he should have played safe by bidding just six notrump, allowing for a misunderstanding. Bidding six and making an overtrick was likely to provide an adequate score.

East was surprised by the auction and asked what it meant. South announced, quite accurately, that they had no agreement about five notrump, and East chose not to double. This was perhaps too cautious: The chance that North–South could make thirteen tricks without playing hearts was very small; and if the grand slam succeeded, East–West would have a disastrous score whether they doubled or not. The same contract would surely not be reached at other tables.

The spade jack was led, and Lawrence was understandably disappointed by the dummy. He was obviously going down, but he had to take into account what was likely to happen at other tables.

He could expect all the rival pairs to reach six notrump, and he could

```
                    NORTH
                    ♠ A 3 2
                    ♡ K Q 3
                    ◇ K J 8
                    ♣ K J 5 3
WEST                                EAST (D)
♠ J 10 9 5                          ♠ 8 7 6
♡ J 8 6 2                           ♡ A 10 4
◇ 6 5 3                             ◇ 9 7 4 2
♣ 4 2                               ♣ 10 8 7
                    SOUTH
                    ♠ K Q 4
                    ♡ 9 7 5
                    ◇ A Q 10
                    ♣ A Q 9 6
```

Both sides were vulnerable.
The bidding:

East	South	West	North
Pass	1 NT	Pass	5 NT
Pass	7 NT	Pass	Pass
Pass			

West led the spade jack.

expect them to fail. He knew something that the other declarers would not know: East held the heart ace, and it was not his curiosity that gave this away. West would obviously have led the ace if he had held it.

So normal play would produce just eleven tricks. And Lawrence could tie that score if he could find a way to make twelve tricks.

He found an ingenious solution by winning the first trick with the spade ace and leading a low heart. He hoped that the heart jack was on his left, and it was. East nervously snatched his ace, which might have been an essential play. The declarer could have held:

```
♠ K Q x
♡ J x
◇ A Q 10 x x
♣ A Q x
```

As it was, South was down one instead of two, and estimated a fair score. He was right, with 10½ match points out of a possible 12. Nobody did better than down one in six notrump, and several went down two when East smoothly ducked the first heart lead to the queen.

South wanted to know why his partner bid five notrump. West wanted to know why his partner had not doubled. "Amazing," comments Lawrence. "We bid a grand and go down, and *no one* is happy."

March 4, 1984

AN INGENIOUS REASON FOR DOUBLING

The reasons that may motivate a player to double are thoroughly documented in bridge literature. Apart from routine penalty and takeout doubles, the latter category including negative and responsive doubles, there are optional doubles, cooperative doubles, negative slam doubles, inhibitory doubles—including the exotic striped-tail ape double—and a variety of lead-directing doubles.

An entirely new and highly ingenious reason for doubling was devised in a deal reported by Ed Pinner. A player often refrains from doubling a contract he knows he can defeat because he fears a successful run-out by his opponents. But in this case the West player recognized that a penalty double represented the best chance of keeping the opponents where he wanted them.

The bidding reached the seven-level with supersonic rapidity. South's wild action, gambling that his partner held the spade ace, was not without some tactical and mathematical justification when East had bid three hearts pre-emptively.

The odds needed to justify a grand slam contract change abruptly when there is a possibility that the opponents will save at favorable vulnerability. A one-in-three chance is good enough if the alternative is to accept a 500 penalty.

On the actual deal, South could see no scientific way of evaluating his grand slam chances, so he shut his eyes and bid seven diamonds. When West saved, not unexpectedly, in seven hearts, North's forcing pass encouraged South to try seven spades. With a hand of lesser quality, North would have doubled seven hearts to discourage his partner.

West was Albert Wolf, a rubber bridge player of great experience. He realized immediately that he could defeat seven spades by giving his partner a diamond ruff: The North–South bidding surely indicated that they held nine diamonds between them.

Superficially, there was no reason to double. The potential profit was trivial, and North–South might take a successful gamble in seven notrump. But as Wolf recognized, the seven notrump possibility was far more likely to eventuate if he failed to double. East would then double seven spades, requesting the unusual diamond lead in accordance with the theory first put forward by Theodore Lightner. West would know what he knew already—that a diamond lead would defeat the contract—but North–South would know it also. Rather than face certain defeat, they would no doubt run to seven notrump.

It was hardly possible for North–South to see through West's imaginative double. It was possible that West held a sure spade trick, in which case seven notrump would be a disaster. So there was no further bidding, and the diamond lead duly defeated the contract.

Seven diamonds and seven notrump would have been unbeatable. In

NORTH (D)
♠ A J 5
♡ A 6
◇ K Q 8 4
♣ J 9 6 2

WEST
♠ 3
♡ K 9 7 4
◇ 9 6 3 2
♣ 10 8 5 3

EAST
♠ 8 6 2
♡ Q J 10 8 5 3 2
◇ —
♣ K Q 7

SOUTH
♠ K Q 10 9 7 4
♡ —
◇ A J 10 7 5
♣ A 4

North and South were vulnerable.
The bidding:

North	East	South	West
1 ◇	3 ♡	7 ◇	7 ♡
Pass	Pass	7 ♠	Dbl.
Pass	Pass	Pass	

West led the diamond two.

seven hearts doubled, East would have lost three or four tricks, according to his handling of the club suit. The unusual winning play of taking two finesses against the jack and nine in the North hand might have been attempted if the early play had marked the major-suit aces in the North hand and therefore the minor-suit aces with South.

January 28, 1980

A MACHIAVELLIAN DECEPTION

The bridge column written by José Le Dentu of Paris in *Le Figaro* has long been regarded as one of the world's best. He recently posed the following question: Should players be expected to retire from serious competitive play on reaching the age of, say, eighty?

Such a suggestion would no doubt provoke roars of rage from three famous Americans, world champions all, who won major national team titles late in life: Sam Stayman, who won at 75; B. Jay Becker, who won at 76; and the late Oswald Jacoby, who won at 80.

In answering his own question in the negative, Le Dentu offered another name: Ado Eichel, age eighty-four. This little-known player competed in a tournament in Cannes and came up with a prize-winning play.

Obviously a grand slam is a good proposition for North–South, but which should be selected? All of them are easy if the clubs behave favorably. If not, what other chances are there? Seven notrump offers a faint chance of a squeeze in the minor suits. Better is seven spades, for the declarer can play two rounds of trumps and then play clubs, guarding against a position in which one defender has length in both black suits.

Both these plans would fail in practice. Seven clubs seems inferior to seven spades, but it does offer a chance of a coup if East has J x x x of trumps. Eichel as South landed in seven clubs after an auction in which spades were not mentioned. The opening club bid was artificial; and when the strong club suit was shown with a jump on the second round, North raised. South made a questionable use of Blackwood and settled in the grand slam. He would have been in considerable difficulties if North had shown one ace rather than two.

West led the spade nine against seven clubs, which was won with the jack in the closed hand. South played the king of clubs followed by the

NORTH
- ♠ Q 10 4
- ♡ A K 7 4
- ◇ A K 6 3
- ♣ K 5

WEST
- ♠ 9 8 5
- ♡ Q 9 6 5 3
- ◇ Q 9 8 2
- ♣ 7

EAST
- ♠ 7 6
- ♡ J 10 8 2
- ◇ J 10 5
- ♣ J 8 3 2

SOUTH (D)
- ♠ A K J 3 2
- ♡ —
- ◇ 7 4
- ♣ A Q 10 9 6 4

Both sides were vulnerable.
The bidding:

South	West	North	East
1 ♣	Pass	1 ♡	Pass
3 ♣	Pass	4 ♣	Pass
4 NT	Pass	5 ♡	Pass
7 ♣	Pass	Pass	Pass

West led the spade nine.

ace, ready to claim his grand slam if everyone followed. But he had to think carefully when West discarded a heart. The position was now this:

NORTH
- ♠ Q 10
- ♡ A K 7 4
- ◇ A K 6 3
- ♣ —

WEST
- ♠ 8 5
- ♡ Q 9 6 5
- ◇ Q 9 8 2
- ♣ —

EAST
- ♠ 7
- ♡ J 10 8 2
- ◇ J 10 5
- ♣ J 8

SOUTH
- ♠ A K 3 2
- ♡ —
- ◇ 7 4
- ♣ Q 10 9 8

South's hope was to maneuver a coup. If he could have the lead in dummy after the eleventh trick while retaining the Q-10 of trumps in his hand, East's trumps would be trapped. In theory he had to find East

49

with three spades. In that case the spade winners could be cashed, and the trumps in the closed hand could be used to ruff two hearts.

As can be seen, this plan was due to fail, since East can ruff the third spade. There was no genuine way to make the grand slam, but Eichel found an ingenious way to throw dust in East's eyes. At the fourth trick, he led to the spade ten, and he then cashed the heart winners in dummy. On these he discarded the ace and king of spades, creating the illusion that he had no more cards in the suit. He had now produced four cards in the unbid spade suit, and East did not suspect a fifth.

So when the spade queen was now led from the dummy, East was not inclined to sacrifice his potential trump trick by ruffing. Instead he discarded a heart, and was surprised to see the declarer follow suit. South now ruffed a heart, crossed to the diamond king, and ruffed another heart. The diamond ace was the final entry to the dummy, and South had achieved his goal. Only two cards remained, East's trumps were trapped, and the grand slam was made. This earned a loud cheer for the eighty-four-year-old declarer, clearly a disciple of Machiavelli.

September 5, 1982

CHAPTER 5
THE LAWS OF THE GAME

Very few players know much about the laws of the game, and even professional directors, as witness the first deal in this section, have been known to err. This relates to repeating a partner's opening bid. We shall also have a historical flashback and an opening lead before the conclusion of the auction. Finally, we have a lead from the right hand that an opponent thinks is wrong, and a partnership that was operating under a most unusual set of laws and regulations.

SIMULTANEOUS BIDDING

Mistaken rulings caused a furor twice in the 1981 Spring National Championships. The first was in the Vanderbilt Cup and the second, on the deal shown in the diagram, was in the Women's Knockout Teams semifinal. North and South were Karen McCallum of New York City and Kitty Bethe of Port Washington, Long Island.

The remarkable auction shown in the diagram does not tell the whole story. The bidding was silent, using bidding boxes, and actually began one spade pass one spade. North failed to notice that her partner had opened and thought that she herself was opening the bidding.

After each opponent had rejected an opportunity to accept the insufficient bid, North was told that her partner would be barred for one round if she bid any number of spades, and for the rest of the auction if she made any other call.

North therefore took the plunge and bid seven spades, certain that she would have no other opportunity to bid. West led the club ace confidently, and North tabled the dummy in a state of abject misery.

"Perhaps your partner can ruff," suggested West consolingly. She was astounded when South came to life, and announced that she would indeed ruff and draw trumps to make the grand slam.

Meanwhile, the tournament director, who was away from the table, was having his moment of misery also. He had discovered that he had misstated the law: North should have been told that she could bid two spades without penalty and that South could draw whatever inferences she chose from this action.

If West had known this, she might well have accepted the one-spade bid and shown her clubs at a high level, with uncertain consequences. The director now ruled that a substitute board be played, but a committee eventually decided that the original results should stand. There was no swing, for the grand slam was bid in the other room by normal means.

Whether the committee decided rightly is arguable, for North–South got rather the best of it: If seven spades had failed, the board would surely have been thrown out.

The moral may be that, since even highly experienced directors do not always quote the law correctly, they should be required to read the law from the law book rather than rely on their memories.

March 31, 1981

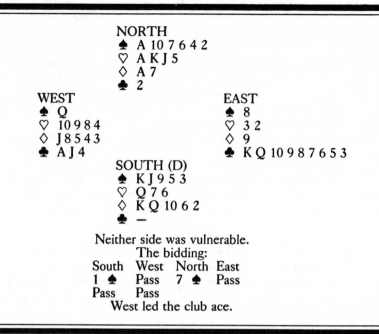

NORTH
♠ A 10 7 6 4 2
♡ A K J 5
♢ A 7
♣ 2

WEST
♠ Q
♡ 10 9 8 4
♢ J 8 5 4 3
♣ A J 4

EAST
♠ 8
♡ 3 2
♢ 9
♣ K Q 10 9 8 7 6 5 3

SOUTH (D)
♠ K J 9 5 3
♡ Q 7 6
♢ K Q 10 6 2
♣ —

Neither side was vulnerable.
The bidding:

South	West	North	East
1 ♠	Pass	7 ♠	Pass
Pass	Pass		

West led the club ace.

THE INFINITE REDOUBLE

At the beginning of the century, before bridge metamorphosed into auction and contract, redoubles were permitted ad infinitum. This made it possible to lose the family farm on a single deal, and the later elimination of multiple redoubles served to limit the sufferings of those blessed with ebullient and wealthy partners.

The original laws might and might not have increased West's sufferings on the diagramed deal, reported from rubber bridge play by the *International Popular Bridge Monthly*, an English publication.

South's direct raise to six hearts was a typical rubber bridge effort, based on the assumption that the partnership did not have the bidding efficiency to reach a sound grand slam. He should have thought about a grand slam force of five notrump. Against seven hearts East would have been hard pressed to find a diamond lead.

North–South had missed a laydown grand slam—but in diamonds, not hearts. East decided, not unreasonably, that there must be a cheap save somewhere and bid six notrump. Better, no doubt, would be a bid of six spades, implying possession of a minor suit since East would have bid directly with a one-suited hand.

As it was, West supposed that his partner had both minor suits. He changed his mind when South moved on to seven diamonds, and persevered to seven spades.

This would have been a cheap save—down just two tricks unless North found a double-dummy underlead of the heart ace to secure a club ruff—but South was not willing to settle for a small penalty. He tried seven notrump, a gamble, and gambled again with a redouble when East doubled.

West knew that he had to lead a black suit, but had no idea which. If his partner's double was a clue, it was a mysterious one. Finally he decided that South must be prepared for a spade lead and tried a club. South happily claimed, and West's choice of lead had cost 5,930 points —surely one of the most expensive in the history of the game.

West was speechless, but East offered words of consolation. "It might have been worse," he pointed out. "Under the old laws I would have given a few more redoubles."

North followed this up with a farsighted thought: "If they bring back those laws," he told South, "we can have a convention. One redouble asks for a club lead, two for diamonds. . . ."

November 11, 1983

NORTH (D)
♠ K 3 2
♡ A Q 9 8 7 4
◇ Q 7 5 2
♣ —

WEST
♠ Q J 10 8 4
♡ 6 3
◇ —
♣ K 10 8 6 4 2

EAST
♠ A 9 7 6 5
♡ 5
◇ 8 6
♣ Q J 9 5 3

SOUTH
♠ —
♡ K J 10 2
◇ A K J 10 9 4 3
♣ A 7

North and South were vulnerable.
The bidding:

North	East	South	West
1 ♡	Pass	6 ♡	Pass
Pass	6 NT	Dbl.	7 ♣
Pass	Pass	7 ◇	7 ♠
Pass	Pass	7 NT	Pass
Pass	Dbl.	Redbl.	Pass
Pass	Pass		

West led the club six.

THE LAW ON ORDER

Leaving aside a small minority of experts, bridge players as a body display a massive ignorance of the laws of their game. This is partly because there are two codes of laws, one for rubber bridge and one for duplicate, and each is highly complex, perhaps more complex than that used in any other sport or recreation. It is doubtful whether anyone in the world could score 100 percent in an examination on bridge law, although Edgar Kaplan of New York would come close.

In a tournament a director is always available to administer the law, but in other situations, in a home or club, a law book should be kept handy for emergencies. Making proper use of the book may not be easy, however, as the players discovered on the diagramed deal played at "The Bridge House."

With each side dominating two suits and voids present in three hands, the auction was sure to reach the slam level, and it did so very quickly. South opened a minimum hand with one heart and was surprised to hear his partner bounce to six hearts over West's takeout double. This was a reasonable gamble designed to put pressure on the opponents, making everyone guess. In tournament play, North might bid four diamonds, a splinter bid showing hopes of a heart slam and shortness, in this case probably a void, in the suit bid.

East tried six spades, and North persevered with seven clubs. West made a rather cowardly decision by doubling, and when the bid came back to South he considered whether to try seven hearts. This was a crucial decision. It can be seen that seven clubs was hopeless on any lead, but seven hearts would succeed if West attempted to cash a diamond trick.

South's thinking was interrupted unexpectedly. Under the delusion that the bidding was over, East led a small diamond. The players turned hopefully to a knowledgeable kibitzer and asked for a ruling. But Barbara Kachmar, winner of many national titles, declined politely to rule on this rare situation, suggesting reference to the law book. This took some time to unearth and even more time to consult.

Eventually the players discovered Law 23 and found that there would have been no penalty, if the card had been dropped accidentally. But as it was a premature lead, West was barred for one round and the diamond three became a penalty card.

South decided to bid seven hearts, partly because he would then have some control over West's opening lead. West might have thought of bidding seven spades, but he was forced to pass. East passed also, for a Lightner double asking for a club lead was not likely to help when South could dictate the lead.

With the exposed card on the table, South could require or forbid a diamond lead. North's original leap to six hearts suggested that he was

```
                      NORTH
                      ♠ 7 3
                      ♡ J 10 8 4 3
                      ◇ —
                      ♣ A Q J 6 5 4
     WEST                               EAST
     ♠ A K 6 2                          ♠ Q J 10 8 4
     ♡ —                                ♡ 9 7 2
     ◇ A K Q 10 5 4                     ◇ J 9 8 3 2
     ♣ 10 9 2                           ♣ —
                      SOUTH (D)
                      ♠ 9 5
                      ♡ A K Q 6 5
                      ◇ 7 6
                      ♣ K 8 7 3
```

Both sides were vulnerable
The bidding: ·

South	West	North	East
1 ♡	Dbl.	6 ♡	6 ♠
Pass	Pass	7 ♣	Pass
Pass	Dbl.	Pass	Pass
7 ♡	Pass	Pass	Pass

West led the spade king.

void in some suit. Not unnaturally, South thought the void would be in spades, and made the disastrous decision of barring a diamond lead, the one thing he needed to make his grand slam.

An inspired club lead would have beaten the contract five, but the defense led spades and took only two tricks. Nobody was very happy in the postmortem, except perhaps the kibitzer. North screamed at South for choosing the wrong penalty, and West screamed at East for leading out of turn.

"If you hadn't done that, I'd have bid seven spades," he insisted, a doubtful claim, since he had not bid over seven clubs, "and we'd have made it."

"No you wouldn't" snapped North. "I'd have made a Lightner double for an unusual lead, and my partner would have led a diamond. Wouldn't you?"

"Of course," responded South, with more confidence than he felt.

January 22, 1976

A DECEPTIVE DIRECTOR

The statement "He who can, plays; he who cannot, directs" is at best a half-truth, like the Shavian maxim about teachers from which it derives. Many directors at the tournament and club level are admittedly ignorant of the finer points of bidding and play, a failing of no great moment in carrying out their duties.

On the rare occasions on which a hesitation situation, for example, calls for expert understanding of bidding, a consultant can usually be found to assist.

As against that, many directors are excellent players and would rank high in the game if their duties permitted. One of these is Jack Hudgins of Nashua, New Hampshire, New England's star director.

Many years ago, on the diagramed deal, he produced an entirely original deceptive play to make a grand slam. It helps to demarcate the line, which as a director he well understands, between legitimate deception and improper trickery.

In guessing a two-way finesse for a queen, for example, players have been known to think for a long time and then lead rapidly from the wrong hand. They expect the defender who objects to have the queen, since he is more interested in the situation than his partner is.

This ploy is a clear impropriety, not because it trades on the reactions of an opponent, which is proper, but because it depends on a deliberate infraction of the laws of the game. The Hudgins coup did not hinge on any misdemeanor and was entirely ethical.

A degree of optimism by his partner carried Hudgins into a grand slam in spades missing the king and another trump. At double-dummy this succeeds 76 percent of the time, but in practice the percentage is 52 percent by playing for the drop, since the opponents do not show their cards.

Hudgins persuaded West to "show" his spade king. When a club was led, he played the club ace from dummy. To the next trick, he led the spade queen from his hand, and West, who had not given the proceedings his full attention, objected.

He thought Hudgins would now have to lead trumps from the dummy, guaranteeing a trick for his king. He was right about the law, but not about the facts, for Hudgins turned his first card, revealing a trump.

It was now clear to him that West held the spade king—he would hardly object to a trump lead from the closed hand holding a small singleton—so the finesse was taken and the grand slam came home.

March 8, 1980

NORTH
♠ A 10 8 3 2
♡ A 7
◇ K 6
♣ A 9 8 6

WEST
♠ K 7
♡ 4 2
◇ 9 8 2
♣ K Q J 5 4 3

EAST
♠ —
♡ J 10 9 8 6 5
◇ J 10 5 3
♣ 10 7 2

SOUTH (D)
♠ Q J 9 6 5 4
♡ K Q 3
◇ A Q 7 4
♣ —

Neither side was vulnerable.
The bidding:

South	West	North	East
1 ♠	3 ♣	4 ♣	Pass
4 ◇	Pass	4 ♡	Pass
5 ♠	Pass	7 ♠	Pass
Pass	Pass		

West led the club king.

KNOWING THE SCORE

Rubber bridge and duplicate play constitute two separate worlds that rarely meet. The only occasion on which die-hard rubber bridge players are opposed to a wide range of duplicate experts is in the unique Rubber Bridge tournament that was organized in Las Vegas in the 1960s by Alfred Sheinwold.

This is unique partly because there is no duplicate element—each hand is played only once—and partly because the prizes are in cash. Those who collect the prize money have the enjoyable problem of explaining this income on their tax returns. The first prize was $10,000.

On one occasion the partnership of Charles Gabriel and Dr. "Cap" Crossley seemed headed for elimination in an early round when they trailed by 1,090, with one deal remaining. Fortunately for them the final deal was as shown opposite.

Six clubs is a fine contract that will succeed if West has the spade ace or if South can locate the heart queen. However, the slam is not easy to reach, and, in normal circumstances, North might content himself with a bid of three notrump in response to three clubs.

But the circumstances were not normal. Both sides knew that North and South could only win the match by bidding and making a grand slam, or by collecting a penalty of 1,100 or more. The normal odds for slam bidding were in abeyance, so North naturally raised to the grand slam. He did not expect his partner to make it, but he wanted to go down fighting.

East prayed for his partner to lead a spade, but his prayers were not answered. Against a grand slam it is usual to look for a safe lead that will give nothing away, and from West's side a heart seemed safest.

The heart four was led and South took East's nine with the ten. He led to the diamond ace, cashed the club ace, and then overtook the club queen with the king. A diamond was ruffed with dummy's remaining trump, and the closed hand was reentered by leading a heart to the ace.

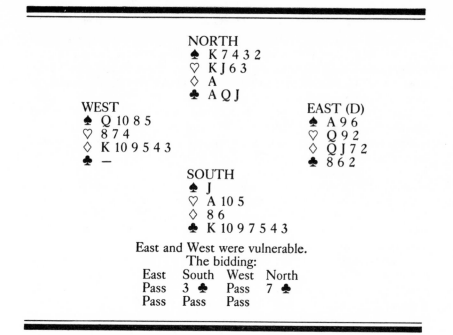

NORTH
♠ K 7 4 3 2
♡ K J 6 3
◇ A
♣ A Q J

WEST
♠ Q 10 8 5
♡ 8 7 4
◇ K 10 9 5 4 3
♣ —

EAST (D)
♠ A 9 6
♡ Q 9 2
◇ Q J 7 2
♣ 8 6 2

SOUTH
♠ J
♡ A 10 5
◇ 8 6
♣ K 10 9 7 5 4 3

East and West were vulnerable.
The bidding:

East	South	West	North
Pass	3 ♣	Pass	7 ♣
Pass	Pass	Pass	

The declarer cashed all his trumps but one, leaving this position:

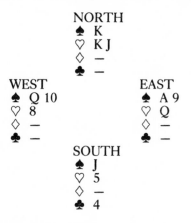

NORTH
♠ K
♡ K J
◇ —
♣ —

WEST
♠ Q 10
♡ 8
◇ —
♣ —

EAST
♠ A 9
♡ Q
◇ —
♣ —

SOUTH
♠ J
♡ 5
◇ —
♣ 4

On the last trump, spades were discarded all around the table. South had to guess at the twelfth trick when he led the heart five and West played the eight.

The opening lead was the clue: If West had started with ◇X 10 8 5 and ◇Q 8 7 4 he would, no doubt, have made the safer-looking lead of a spade. So Crossley put up the king in dummy, made his grand slam, and won the match.

East was criticized rather unfairly for failing to open one spade, a bid which would have guided his partner to the right lead against the expected grand slam contract. Such an exercise of the imagination would have been more likely to lead to a 1,100 penalty than to successful defense against a grand slam.

Notice that a sacrifice in seven diamonds would not quite have saved the day for East–West. Even with the winning guess in the spade suit, the penalty would have been 1,100, and they would have lost the match by the smallest possible margin.

November 12, 1967

CHAPTER 6

A RUBBER AT THE CLUB

There is a major difference between club bridge in North America and the European equivalent. On this side of the Atlantic, four-deal bridge, or Chicago, has become standard. Elsewhere the traditional rubber, which can drag on to the annoyance of those waiting to cut in, remains the norm.

Four of the five deals in this chapter are from rubber bridge. One involves members of the world's most famous fictional club, the Griffins, created by Victor Mollo.

Sims Was the Great Psychologist

Howard Schenken has met all the greats of the game, both at the table and away from it, and is in the view of many the greatest of them all. He and his teammates in the thirties, the Four Aces, clearly outclassed Ely Culbertson in competition, but never achieved the public reputation they deserved.

On the diagramed deal, played in a high-stake rubber bridge game some forty years ago, Schenken was kibitzing that colorful personality, P. Hal Sims, whose home in Deal, New Jersey, always was crowded with the game's leading players. Bidding methods were somewhat crude in those days, and North–South reached seven notrump in three bids.

Most modern players would open the North hand with two notrump and reach a comfortable six notrump. Seven clubs is an acceptable contract, needing only a three–two trump break, but seven notrump was distinctly optimistic. On the face of it, Sims, as South, needed to find not only a three–two club split, but also to collect the spade jack.

Both these chances were destined to fail, as can be seen. There was a faint chance of a squeeze, and as it happens this could have succeeded, since East held all the missing major-suit honors. But Sims's forte was psychology rather than technique, and he chose another road.

He cashed all his high-card winners, in this order: spade queen; ace, king, and queen of diamonds, throwing a heart; spade ace and king; ace, king, queen of clubs, and ace and king of hearts. The lead was now in dummy, and East could see this:

NORTH
♠ —
♡ 9
♢ —
♣ 3

EAST
♠ J
♡ Q
♢ —
♣ —

The club three was led, from dummy, and put East to the test. He knew that South still had the spade ten and a club. But which club? Too late, East realized that he should have been watching the spots.

Finally he decided on general principles that South must have the winning club, and let go the heart queen. But Sims triumphantly produced the club deuce, and made the last trick in the dummy with the heart nine.

Notice that this was purely a rubber bridge coup. By pulling cards apparently at random from the dummy, Sims had managed to dispose of

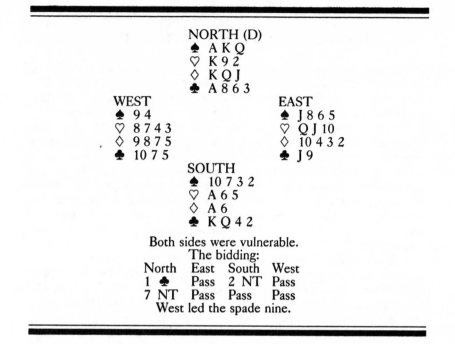

NORTH (D)
♠ A K Q
♡ K 9 2
◇ K Q J
♣ A 8 6 3

WEST
♠ 9 4
♡ 8 7 4 3
◇ 9 8 7 5
♣ 10 7 5

EAST
♠ J 8 6 5
♡ Q J 10
◇ 10 4 3 2
♣ J 9

SOUTH
♠ 10 7 3 2
♡ A 6 5
◇ A 6
♣ K Q 4 2

Both sides were vulnerable.
The bidding:

North	East	South	West
1 ♣	Pass	2 NT	Pass
7 NT	Pass	Pass	Pass

West led the spade nine.

the eight and six of clubs under his king-queen. At duplicate, he would have had to instruct his partner to play the right club spots, and East would automatically have been alerted to the significance of the small clubs.

November 15, 1973

COMIC DEFENSE HAS SERIOUS RESULT

When a declarer is in an easy contract, it is sometimes possible to throw him off balance by doing something unexpected, even weird. Perhaps the most brilliant example of this occurred on the diagramed deal, played many years ago in a rubber bridge game for high stakes.

The hero was Andy Gabrilovich of Stamford, Connecticut, and the scene was Crockfords Club in London, a famous institution that has since reverted to less intellectual forms of gambling.

The excellent contract of seven spades was reached in the English style, starting with a four-card major opening. Some experts would treat the four notrump bid after three notrump as a natural invitation, but there was no misunderstanding. South responded to both stages of Blackwood, and North bid the grand slam after locating two aces and three kings.

It is clear that the contract presents no problem. South can ruff a heart in the dummy, draw trumps, and eventually score four club tricks. But a funny thing happened on the way to the postmortem. When he ruffed his heart loser at the third trick, Gabrilovich, as East, had to make a discard. And his discard was, of all things, a trump—an underruff.

This pulled up South dead in his tracks. What possible reason could East have for discarding a trump? The only explanation seemed to be that he had some protection in each minor suit and could not afford a discard in either.

Satisfied with this analysis, South decided to play Gabrilovich for four clubs headed by the jack. He began by cashing his A–K in diamonds, just in case the queen fell. Then he led to the spade king and led a club to the nine.

If the cards had been lying as South believed, this would have been the right way to make thirteen tricks. But then the roof fell in. West produced the club jack, and the defense added insult to injury by taking a diamond trick.

Gabrilovich's underruffing joke had served to defeat a "laydown" grand slam by two tricks.

April 14, 1980

NORTH
- ♠ K 10 9 7
- ♡ A 4
- ◇ J 3 2
- ♣ A Q 10 3

WEST
- ♠ 3
- ♡ Q J 9 8 7 3
- ◇ 9 7 5 4
- ♣ J 6

EAST
- ♠ 6 5 4 2
- ♡ 10 2
- ◇ Q 10 8
- ♣ 8 5 4 2

SOUTH (D)
- ♠ A Q J 8
- ♡ K 6 5
- ◇ A K 6
- ♣ K 9 7

Both sides were vulnerable.
The bidding:

South	West	North	East
1 ♠	Pass	2 ♣	Pass
3 NT	Pass	4 NT	Pass
5 ♡	Pass	5 NT	Pass
6 ♠	Pass	7 ♠	Pass
Pass	Pass		

West led the heart queen.

TEMPESTS AT THE TABLE

It is commonly believed, especially by those who know only the hurly-burly of the tournament world, that card clubs are oases of peace and quiet. Courtesy and harmony prevail, it is thought, and harsh words are never spoken.

This is no doubt true of some clubs, but over the years there have been some conspicuous exceptions. In 1825, in London, Stratford Club dissolved itself as the only way to exclude a highly disagreeable member. Reconstituted as the Portland Club, it eventually became the lawmaking body for bridge. In 1836, England's premier baron, Baron de Ros, unsuccessfully sued some fellow members of Grahams Club in London because they had accused him of cheating at whist. In 1890, one Joseph Pike in Cork, Ireland, won a libel suit relating to a charge that he had cheated at poker, perhaps because the judge had been heavily bribed by the plaintiff's mother.

In this century, bridge clubs have been in turmoil for quite different reasons. Some have been raided by zealous policemen seeking to prevent illegal gambling; but this practice declined when various courts ruled that bridge is a game of skill. In 1982, two episodes were widely discussed.

A routine skip-bid warning triggered a brouhaha that sent ripples through the New York bridge world. And in Philadelphia a dispute between the estranged proprietors of a small club escalated. While one of them was conducting a duplicate game, the other organized a noisy party on the floor above. The local bridge organization, after considerable thought, suspended the party host for six months. The decision was reversed on a first appeal but sustained on a further appeal to the national authority. The host then started a suit against the American Contract Bridge League.

Fictional clubs are not immune from such developments. The players at Victor Mollo's famous Griffins Club often have to resort to committees for arbitration and there is daily exasperation. Much of this stems from the open gloating of the Hideous Hog for which he makes no apologies: "Maybe I gloat more than others do, but isn't that simply because I win more and am reluctant, being sociable by nature, to keep my little triumphs to myself? The occasional jeer, the odd whoop or two, are only intended to bring out the finer points of play which might otherwise escape attention."

The Hog had his gloating turned up to full volume after the diagramed deal described in *Bridge in the Fourth Dimension*. He held the South cards, and listened while his opponents bid to seven diamonds. This was a sound contract, but it was due to be defeated by a heart lead and the Hog knew it. He also knew that if he passed, his partner was likely to make a Lightner double, calling for the heart lead and so scare the opponents into seven hearts.

```
                    NORTH
                    ♠ 9 8 7 6 5
                    ♡ —
                    ◇ 6
                    ♣ Q J 10 9 4 3 2
WEST (D)                                    EAST
♠ —                                         ♠ K J
♡ A K J 10 9                                ♡ Q 8 7
◇ K 10 8 7 5 4                              ◇ A Q J 9
♣ 6 5                                       ♣ A K 8 7
                    SOUTH
                    ♠ A Q 10 4 3 2
                    ♡ 6 5 4 3 2
                    ◇ 3 2
                    ♣ —
```

East and West were vulnerable.
The bidding:

West	North	East	South
1 ♡	Pass	3 ◇	Pass
4 ◇	Pass	4 ♡	Pass
4 ♠	Pass	5 ♣	Pass
5 NT	Pass	7 ◇	Dbl.
7 ♡	Pass	Pass	7 ♠
Dbl.	Pass	Pass	Pass

West led the heart ace.

He, therefore, doubled directly, preventing the tip-off, but to his annoyance West retreated to seven hearts. He knew this would be defeated
by a black-suit lead, but his partner, the Rueful Rabbit, was quite capa-
ble of leading a disastrous diamond. To avert a possible big loss, the Hog
bid seven spades, prepared to accept a small penalty. He knew he would
be able to ruff some hearts in the dummy.

West naturally doubled seven spades, and could have taken a trick by
leading a diamond. Not unnaturally, however, he supposed that there
was a diamond void somewhere. He led the heart ace, which was ruffed
in dummy. The Hog led the club queen to ruff out one high club honor
and returned to dummy with a heart ruff to repeat the process. When he
ruffed another heart and led club winners, East was helpless. Sooner or
later his trumps would be eliminated.

After the score for making seven spades doubled had been calculated,
the Hog's gloating began, and it continued as long as anyone was prepared to listen.

August 22, 1982

Planning Ahead in Bidding Can Lead
to New Sequence

Planning ahead in the bidding can sometimes cause an expert to abandon routine paths and emerge with a startling sequence. A prize for imaginative bidding ought to go to John Percy of New York for his effort on the diagramed deal played at the Gallerie of Bridge and Games, 345 East 80 Street.

North–South were playing all two-bids as strong, but Percy, as South, rejected a two-heart bid. Instead, he bid two diamonds, judging that this would be the best way to find out whether his partner held the A-Q of that suit, the two key cards.

When North jumped to four diamonds, South used the grand-slam force. North dutifully bid seven diamonds, showing two of the top three diamond honors and making West a happy man.

The happiness was purely temporary, however, for South naturally converted to seven hearts. The situation was now clear to the other players: South must have a monster heart suit and a secondary diamond suit lacking two top honors.

Looking at the North–South hands, seven hearts is clearly an ideal contract. But it became less ideal when East doubled. East was a player who knew what he was doing, so the double was Lightner.

East was demanding an unusual diamond lead, so he must be void in that suit. But Percy was not inclined to resign himself to immediate defeat, so he converted boldly to seven notrump. He was gambling on the location of the club ace. If West held that card, he was headed for instant defeat; if North held it, South could count on an instant victory. If East held the crucial card, everything would hinge on West's opening lead.

East doubled seven notrump, though with some misgivings. This strongly suggested that he held an ace, but West had no way to know that it was in clubs. Not unnaturally, West led the spade king, fearing that a club lead might give away a trick.

The spade lead gave the declarer a double pleasure. Not only was it not the fatal club he had feared, but it also opened the door to acquiring the thirteenth trick. The bidding had marked West with all the diamonds, and the lead with the spade queen. So South took the spade ace and ran all his hearts, knowing that West would be in trouble.

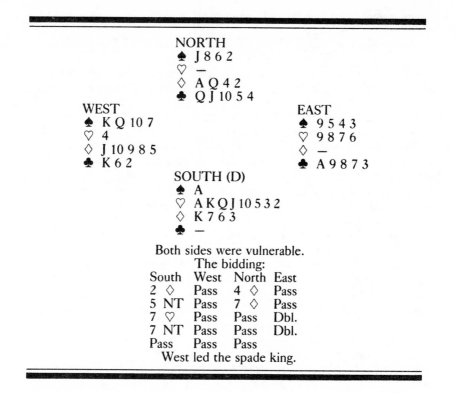

NORTH
♠ J 8 6 2
♡ —
◇ A Q 4 2
♣ Q J 10 5 4

WEST
♠ K Q 10 7
♡ 4
◇ J 10 9 8 5
♣ K 6 2

EAST
♠ 9 5 4 3
♡ 9 8 7 6
◇ —
♣ A 9 8 7 3

SOUTH (D)
♠ A
♡ A K Q J 10 5 3 2
◇ K 7 6 3
♣ —

Both sides were vulnerable.
The bidding:

South	West	North	East
2 ◇	Pass	4 ◇	Pass
5 NT	Pass	7 ◇	Pass
7 ♡	Pass	Pass	Dbl.
7 NT	Pass	Pass	Dbl.
Pass	Pass	Pass	

West led the spade king.

The ending was as follows:

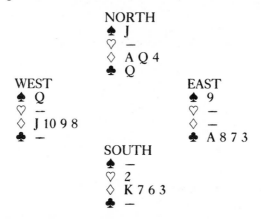

NORTH
♠ J
♡ —
◇ A Q 4
♣ Q

WEST
♠ Q
♡ —
◇ J 10 9 8
♣ —

EAST
♠ 9
♡ —
◇ —
♣ A 8 7 3

SOUTH
♠ —
♡ 2
◇ K 7 6 3
♣ —

On the last heart, West surrendered, since any discard would give the declarer his thirteenth trick. Notice that the same squeeze would have been available had West, foolishly, chosen an opening lead in a red suit.

July 14, 1975

A MINOR BREAKDOWN IN COMMUNICATIONS

Old adages seldom hold good in a bridge context. Those who believe, for example, that truth is stranger than fiction, should study the diagramed deal. It was constructed, in order to set a world record, by Alec Traub of Cape Town, South Africa, an ingenious hand creator and author of books on bridge mathematics.

The scene, says Traub, is a men's rubber bridge game in a local club backwater where strong two-bids are the standard fare. There is no agreement, however, about four notrump bids. North, old and garrulous, favors Roman Blackwood. South, old and slightly deaf, expects his partners to use the Culbertson 4–5 notrump convention.

After some typical gossip from North, South is persuaded that it is his turn to bid. Sounding a little puzzled, he initiates the weird auction shown in the diagram. The explanation of South's bidding will have to wait, but North's actions are explicable. He thinks his partner has shown three aces and two kings in a balanced hand, so there should be thirteen laydown tricks with something to spare. Fearing that something has gone wrong, however, he does not redouble. East, who has been biding his time in the certainty that his opponents are in the grip of a misunderstanding, expects a massive penalty.

After a lead in one of the pointed suits East would indeed have taken the first eight tricks, scoring 2,300 points. Unfortunately for the defense, West stops himself as he's about to make a normal spade lead and asks himself what the double means. He concludes that it is a Lightner double asking for the lead of dummy's suit, so he carefully tables the heart queen.

South seems astonished by the appearance of the dummy, but pulls himself together and calls for the heart ace. When the king falls he runs eight more heart winners and reaches this position:

```
                    NORTH
                    ♠ 10
                    ♡ 3
                    ♢ 10
                    ♣ 2
        WEST                    EAST
        ♠ 9                     ♠ A
        ♡ —                     ♡ —
        ♢ —                     ♢ A
        ♣ 7 6 4                 ♣ K Q
                    SOUTH
                    ♠ —
                    ♡ —
                    ♢ —
                    ♣ A 9 8 5
```

NORTH
♠ 10
♡ A J 10 9 8 7 6 5 4 3
♢ 10
♣ 2

WEST
♠ 9 6 5 4 3
♡ Q
♢ 9 7 6
♣ 7 6 4 3

EAST
♠ A K Q J
♡ K
♢ A K Q J
♣ K Q J 10

SOUTH (D)
♠ 8 7 2
♡ 2
♢ 8 5 4 3 2
♣ A 9 8 5

North and South were vulnerable.
The bidding:

South	West	North	East
2 NT	Pass	3 ♡	Pass
3 NT	Pass	4 NT	Pass
5 ♣	Pass	5 NT	Pass
6 ♡	Pass	7 NT	Dbl.
Pass	Pass	Pass	

West led the heart queen.

When the final heart was led from dummy, East was in extremis. If he had thrown a club, South would have made the rest of the tricks in the closed hand. He postponed the evil day by throwing the spade ace—the diamond ace would have been no better—and his ruin was complete when the spade ten was led from the dummy.

The scoring and the postmortem were quite lengthy. North and South, working away separately with pencil and paper, eventually agreed on a total of 2,690. In the meantime, their opponents had plenty to say.

"You could have led any other suit, partner," fumed East, "and beaten the contract. Even a club lead beats it by two tricks."

"I was going to lead a spade," retorted West, "but your double asked for a heart lead. Why did you double if you couldn't stand a heart lead?"

"Are you suggesting I didn't have a double?" was the response in a strangled scream.

South was in a mellow mood and offered to buy everyone drinks at the bar to celebrate his world record: seven notrump bid and made with a partnership holding of nine high-card points. And eventually the mystery of the opening bid was revealed.

South's deafness had had a curious impact. He thought that his partner had opened out of turn with a strong two-bid and that East had condoned it. Before the start of the deal North had been announcing the triumph of his actress granddaughter in the London theater: She had been offered TWO PARTS.

February 24, 1980

CHAPTER 7

FICTION

It is my firm belief, newspaper accounts to the contrary, that a thirteen-card suit, and a fortiori four thirteen-card suits, does not exist in the real world. The first deal in this section has a thirteen-card suit and was played in a competition—but it was a competition with constructed deals. In the last two deals, I stray into the role of drama critic.

IS BRIDGE LEGAL?

Law and disorder are not usually matters of direct concern to bridge players, but one club proprietor has had significant experience in this area.

On September 17, 1972, the home of Mrs. Madeline Anderson in Seattle was invaded by 12 armed policemen. The 14 bridge players present were taken to a police station, fingerprinted, photographed, and booked on a charge of common gambling.

The patrons of Mrs. Anderson's club, which she has run for some 35 years, are mainly duplicate players. Some rubber bridge is played almost entirely at the minuscule stake of "a tenth," or a dime per hundred.

In the subsequent court hearing, a detective from the Seattle vice control division testified that he had previously visited the club, played with a colleague, and lost a combined total of $3.40.

A Municipal Court judge dismissed the case, basing his decision on a California precedent ruling that bridge is not a game of chance.

The prosecutor then pressed a felony charge against Mrs. Anderson, for "giving aid in the playing of bridge with cards." This was brought under a State of Washington statute legalizing charitable bingo and incidentally setting penalties for other forms of gambling. Another judge then ruled this statute unconstitutional.

The expert witness for the defense was Alfred Sheinwold, who described the case in full in *Popular Bridge*. He was ready to demonstrate that skill is predominant in bridge not only in a session, or in a four-deal cycle of Chicago bridge, but even in a single deal.

It could be contended that even an untutored beginner would need no skill on some deals: He would know what to do, for example, if he picked up a thirteen-card suit. As a counter on this point, Sheinwold cited the diagramed deal, which was constructed in 1932 and played worldwide in the Bridge Olympics promoted by the Culbertson organization.

North usually opened one club, and East stared at his thirteen-card suit in astonishment. The inexperienced East players, correctly assessing that they could make a grand slam, jumped confidently to seven hearts. And in doing so they made a strategic error.

South now worked out that East's extraordinary bid must be based on a thirteen-card suit. With the vulnerability against him he must have solid ground for expecting to make thirteen tricks, and in view of North's opening it was hardly possible that East held twelve hearts and the club ace.

So the imaginative South players—one of whom was the late Harold Vanderbilt, inventor of contract bridge—bid seven notrump and had no trouble making it. There were thirteen top tricks on any lead, and the North–South grand slam would have been made even if North had held the spade queen instead of the king. The declarer would have cashed the spade ace and run diamonds to squeeze West in the black suits.

NORTH (D)
♠ K J 5 2
♡ —
♢ 9 7 6 5
♣ A K 7 5 3

WEST
♠ Q 10 9 7 6 3
♡ —
♢ 4 3
♣ 10 9 6 4 2

EAST
♠ —
♡ A K Q J 10 9
8 7 6 5 4 3 2
♢ —
♣ —

SOUTH
♠ A 8 4
♡ —
♢ A K Q J 10 8 2
♣ Q J 8

East and West were vulnerable.
The bidding:

North	East	South	West
1 ♣	7 ♡	7 NT	Pass
Pass	Pass		

West led the diamond four.

The right strategy for East, with the "simple" thirteen-card hand, has been argued by experts. Some have suggested a one-heart overcall or even a super-cunning pass. Perhaps better still would be to bid four hearts, adding an air of plausibility to later bids of five, six, and seven hearts. And in the unlikely event that East is left to play four hearts, he has at least made a positive score.

April 10, 1972

Jameson's Raid

Whether to finesse or play for the drop is often a crucial decision and may make a difference of several tricks. The maximum in this connection is thirteen tricks, and such a deal was once described in the South African *Bridge Bulletin* by Norreys Davis of Kitwe.

The South player, we are told, was a certain Jameson. He ran the full gamut from mild surprise to total astonishment in a few seconds. First he picked up an 8-4-1-0 freak distribution; then he heard his partner open with a strong artificial bid of two clubs; and last he heard his right-hand opponent, a cautious bidder, jump swiftly and confidently to seven spades.

Knowing that East had never taken a gamble in his life, South worked it out. East must surely have twelve spades and an ace. Eleven spades and an ace–king on the side was hardly possible, for North would not have enough for a forcing two-club opening. As this was rubber bridge for high stakes, South took a little time for arithmetic.

If he passed, the opposition would score 2,360, including 150 for honors. What would happen if he bid seven notrump? This would no doubt be doubled and would go down 3,800 if West managed to lead to his partner's side ace. But if West did not find the right lead, and he had on the face of it one chance in three, North–South would make a lot of tricks. The effect would be a worthwhile sacrifice, and seven notrump might even succeed.

So Jameson screwed his courage to the bidding point and tried seven notrump. East, whose name was Benson, doubled firmly and attempted to calculate the score for down thirteen tricks vulnerable.

Luckily for the declarer, West made an ill-judged opening lead. As he was short in clubs, he reasoned that the club ace was the most likely one for his partner to hold. He should have reflected that if East held the club ace he would make it in any event, since North–South must have clubs in large quantities. A heart lead was indicated, because the heart ace was the one that might fail to score if it were not led.

Jameson was astonished to see the spade king in the dummy: That was a card that he was sure East held, and his calculations had gone astray. East must have eleven spades, the heart ace, and another card, perhaps the club king. He had clearly made a most untypical bid when he jumped to seven spades, and seven notrump was in danger of becoming the most expensive sacrifice of all time.

Next South gazed suspiciously at the club four which West had led. Was this a routine attempt to hit East's ace? Or a cunning play from a doubleton king aimed at discouraging South from finessing? Or a misconception based on the thought that East's double was an attempt to direct a lead in dummy's artificial club suit?

East's bid was perhaps slightly more likely with a small heart rather

```
                    NORTH (D)
                    ♠ K
                    ♡ K Q J 10
                    ◇ A K Q 10 5
                    ♣ A 3 2
WEST                                    EAST
♠ —                                     ♠ A K Q J 10 9
♡ 9 8 7 6 5 4 3 2                         8 7 6 5 4 3
◇ 9 8 7 6                               ♡ A
♣ 4                                     ◇ —
                                        ♣ —
                    SOUTH
                    ♠ 2
                    ♡ —
                    ◇ J 4 3 2
                    ♣ Q J 10 9 8 7 6 5
```
Both sides were vulnerable.
The bidding:

North	East	South	West
2 ♣	7 ♠	7 NT	Pass
Pass	Dbl.	Pass	Pass
Pass			

West led the club four.

than the club king. As against that the play of the club ace meant down seven tricks at worst. Then Jameson had a further thought.

"Luckily," he reported later, "I remembered something else about Benson. He was very vain, and would not admit that he needed glasses. Suddenly the explanation of his extraordinary bid dawned on me. He thought he had twelve spades and the ace of hearts. I put up my club ace, and Benson discarded a low spade. He nearly had apoplexy when I requested him to correct his revoke by playing the club king which was concealed among his spade honors. But he complied."

Speaking legalistically, South's acuteness gained him 3,890 points. If East had been allowed to complete his revoke, South would have been down five, with no legal redress at rubber bridge.

Note: This last sentence is no longer valid. The 1981 Laws say that "Any established revoke . . . causes damage to the nonoffending side insufficiently compensated by this law, the offending side should . . . transfer additional tricks so as to restore equity."

June 9, 1974

NAILING THE OPPOSITION

The cosmetics industry may make a substantial impact on the bridge scene if one of its products becomes popular. Consider the effect on partners, opponents, and tournament committees of a mood crystal nail polish that "changes color in reaction to your body chemistry, revealing true emotional involvement and awareness."

Imagine a home game between two couples in which the wives are both wearing moody nail polish. We'll call them Mr. and Mrs. Culbertson and Mr. and Mrs. Sims, although their skill does not quite match that of the more famous players of the same name who clashed in a celebrated rubber bridge match more than forty years ago. The climax of the evening is the diagramed deal, noted in real life by New York expert Murray Schnee.

The early deals in the final rubber have been routine, but the nails in South and West seats change rapidly from shimmering apricot (indifferent, aloof, nonchalant) to peach mist (emotionally stimulated, interested, alert) when they examine their distributional holdings.

Mrs. Sims, as West, shifts again to copper ice (happy, attentive, and eager) when she hears her husband bid one spade: Seven-card support for partner's major suit and obvious slam possibilities. Mrs. Culbertson as South considers a dramatic jump to five clubs but, as she is vulnerable, contents herself with four.

West now likes her slam prospects better, for East's high cards seem to be in the red suits rather than clubs. She bids five clubs, suggesting strong spade support, control of clubs, and slam interest. North jams the bidding further with a bid of six clubs and East has nothing to say. Since his queen–jack of clubs were probably worthless, his hand looks quite weak.

West, still flashing copper ice from the hand holding her cards, continues to six spades. North thinks about doubling but realizes that he is not on lead. If his partner does not find a diamond lead, he thinks the slam might succeed. As it happens, he is wrong about this: Six spades is due to fail on any lead, even a low club. But if East holds a singleton diamond instead of a doubleton, the slam would be a laydown. So North passes, leaving the decision about whether to sacrifice to his partner, who decides that her hand will not contribute to the defense. South bids seven clubs to West's annoyance. She passes the final decision to East, who doubles: He feels confident that neither side can make thirteen tricks.

West considers the opening lead, and her nails turn to lime frost (apprehensive, anxious, excited, nervous). Leading away from one of the red queens might give away a crucial trick, so she puts the spade ace on the table.

The ruff-and-sluff on opening lead sets a small trap for South, who, in her turn, is now showing copper ice (happy, attentive, eager). The third

NORTH
♠ —
♡ J 10 6 4
◇ A K 10 7 5 2
♣ 10 7 2

WEST
♠ A K 10 9 7 5 4
♡ Q 7 2
◇ Q 8 4
♣ —

EAST (D)
♠ Q J 8 6 3 2
♡ A K 3
◇ J 6
♣ Q J

SOUTH
♠ —
♡ 9 8 5
◇ 9 3
♣ A K 9 8 6 5 4 3

Both sides were vulnerable.
The bidding:

East	South	West	North
1 ♠	4 ♣	5 ♣	6 ♣
Pass	Pass	6 ♠	Pass
Pass	7 ♣	Pass	Pass
Dbl.	Pass	Pass	Pass

West led the spade ace.

club in dummy is needed as an entry, so she ruffs in her hand, draws trumps, and establishes diamonds with a third-round ruff. The club ten is now the entry, and three losing hearts are discarded on three winning diamonds.

"Why didn't you lead a heart?" screams Sims, signaling his own mood with a face that has turned purple. "We'd have made the first three tricks."

"I would have if you had made the obvious lead-directing bid of six hearts," screams back his spouse, whose nails have turned a peculiar shade unplanned by the manufacturers.

"I make that 2,330," announces North after a little work with a pocket calculator.

South says nothing, but her nails have turned bronze orchid: passionate, romantic, warm, satisfied.

March 20, 1977

ANNIE BID YOUR SLAM

For the five thousand players who traveled to Fresno, California, for the 1980 Spring Nationals, a well-organized tournament with unsurpassed local hospitality, the most delightful feature was a theatrical performance. It was *Annie Bid Your Slam,* a modified version of a famous Broadway show, produced and written by Peter Rank, who has long been one of the best West Coast players and here revealed that his talents lie in many directions.

Anne Doubly and her three farming sisters arrive to play in their first tournament, bringing their own table and chairs. Having full faith in "biddin' what comes naturally," they reach the last round of the Swiss Teams tied with a men's foursome from New York headed by Frank Scientific.

Annie's bidding and play are of the shotgun variety, as she demonstrates on the diagramed deal, which was projected on to a side wall for the benefit of the audience. When she opens one notrump one of her sisters raises directly to seven notrump, a reasonable shot. Some North players would use Gerber to make sure that the partnership is not missing an ace, but the Doubly family is used to playing without conventions.

When the dummy appears, Anne quickly counts twelve tricks and announces that she will take a diamond finesse for the thirteenth trick. This brings home the slam, and the spotlight moves to the other table where this is the final deal. Frank's team has the lead, and he will win if he duplicates the grand slam result. He and his partner embark on eight rounds of sophisticated bidding, announcing alerts at every turn and thereby mystifying their opponents.

Frank's teammates, who have finished playing against Annie, are now center stage conversing nervously. "If we are to win," says one, "Frank has to reach seven notrump and misplay it." He then explains just why Annie's decision to finesse in diamonds is technically inferior. South can and should take the diamond ace and all his winners outside the diamond suit, taking care to wind up in the South hand at the finish. When he leads toward dummy at the twelfth trick, with one diamond and one club in his hand he can count the original distribution. He knows that West began with five spades, four hearts, one club, and, therefore, three diamonds. East must have begun with four diamonds, and so is more likely than not to have begun with the queen.

East has one club winner left, and, therefore, only one of his diamonds. If he had the queen, he has been squeezed in the minor suits and the queen will fall. So Frank leads to the king and goes down. He has made the technically perfect play, but Annie has won. She and her sisters are jubilant.

Annie and Frank discover that falling in love is wonderful, and he recruits her as his partner for the tournament circuit on the clear under-

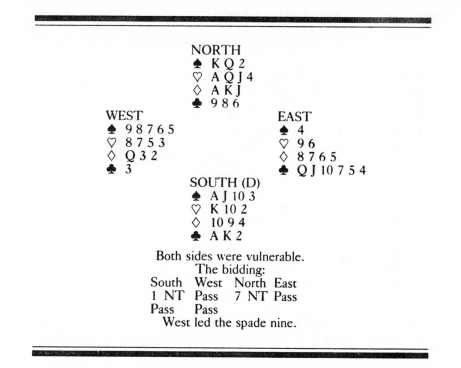

NORTH
♠ K Q 2
♡ A Q J 4
◇ A K J
♣ 9 8 6

WEST
♠ 9 8 7 6 5
♡ 8 7 5 3
◇ Q 3 2
♣ 3

EAST
♠ 4
♡ 9 6
◇ 8 7 6 5
♣ Q J 10 7 5 4

SOUTH (D)
♠ A J 10 3
♡ K 10 2
◇ 10 9 4
♣ A K 2

Both sides were vulnerable.
The bidding:

South	West	North	East
1 NT	Pass	7 NT	Pass
Pass	Pass		

West led the spade nine.

standing that she follows his methods and lets him play all the hands. They win the Life Master Pair Championship, but she has had a reversion to her bouncy bidding methods and he leaves her in dismay.

But there is no business like bridge business and there is a happy ending when he finds that "My defenses are down . . . being vulnerable is gonna be fun." The lyric seems about to conclude with a famous New York expert, but it turns out to be the nineteenth-century inventor of the standard movement for a duplicate game:
"Like a clubless Howard Schenken,
Like Stayman in one notrump,
Like Blackwood without a slam bid,
Like Mitchell without his bump."

April 13, 1980

ELIZA BIDLITTLE DOESN'T

A few years back, Rex Harrison made a triumphant Broadway return, after more than twenty years, as Professor Henry Higgins in the revival of Lerner and Loewe's *My Fair Lady.*

Not long after, a similar production was revived at the Sheraton-Palace Hotel in San Francisco, before an equally enthusiastic if smaller audience. It was *My Fair (Little Old) Lady,* first produced by Peter Rank in 1966 and then updated and improved by him.

Henry Huddle, a superior bridge expert, decides to take the worst player in the local game and teach her everything he knows. Her name is Eliza Bidlittle, and her natural tendency is to say ''pass'' whenever it is her turn—even if her partner has made a cue-bid.

Not unexpectedly, he finds it very hard work (''Poor Henry Huddle''), but eventually she understands how to be a winner: ''Close Games, Sound Slams, and Careful Dummy Play'' to the tune of ''The Rain in Spain.'' Meanwhile, another expert draws boos from a section of the audience by demanding to know: ''Why can't a woman play like a man?''

Finally, they are ready for the Nationals (''Everyone who should be here is here''), and when they reach the last deal of the Blue Ribbon Pair Championship, shown in the diagram, they are in contention for the title.

Huddle's temporizing response of two clubs to one spade was distinctly dubious; when he followed with a jump to three spades, Eliza was naturally bullish about slam possibilities. Expecting to find a long club suit in the dummy, she contracted for seven spades after finding that the partnership held all the aces.

The analytically minded spectators, who were given the deal to think about while waiting for the show to start, could see that a neutral lead, such as a trump, would allow the slam to be made. South can discard a heart on the third round of diamonds, ruff the second round of hearts, and eventually squeeze East in hearts and clubs.

But for this squeeze to operate, South must be able to get to and fro in clubs. So, the actual club lead defeats the slam. Or does it? Just as a kibitzing expert announces that ''there is no possible way to bring home the slam. She'll get what she deserves for her wild and illogical bidding,'' Eliza confounds him by rising from the table with a triumphant cry: ''Making seven!''

How did she do it? She played low from dummy and captured the jack

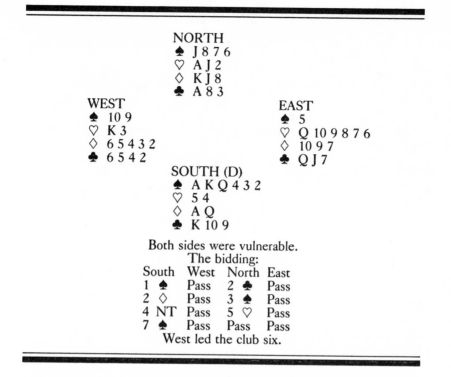

NORTH
♠ J 8 7 6
♡ A J 2
◇ K J 8
♣ A 8 3

WEST
♠ 10 9
♡ K 3
◇ 6 5 4 3 2
♣ 6 5 4 2

EAST
♠ 5
♡ Q 10 9 8 7 6
◇ 10 9 7
♣ Q J 7

SOUTH (D)
♠ A K Q 4 3 2
♡ 5 4
◇ A Q
♣ K 10 9

Both sides were vulnerable.
The bidding:

South	West	North	East
1 ♠	Pass	2 ♣	Pass
2 ◇	Pass	3 ♠	Pass
4 NT	Pass	5 ♡	Pass
7 ♠	Pass	Pass	Pass

West led the club six.

with the king. She then cashed just five rounds of trumps and two diamond winners, overtaking with the king to have the lead in dummy in this position:

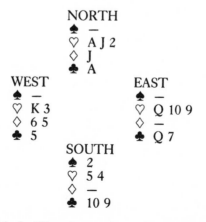

NORTH
♠ —
♡ A J 2
◇ J
♣ A

WEST
♠ —
♡ K 3
◇ 6 5
♣ 5

EAST
♠ —
♡ Q 10 9
◇ —
♣ Q 7

SOUTH
♠ 2
♡ 5 4
◇ —
♣ 10 9

On the diamond jack, Eliza threw a heart from her hand and watched to see what East would discard. That player was helpless. If he threw a club, South would cash the club ace. So, he threw a heart and South played hearts next. A ruff established dummy's jack, and the club ace was still there as an entry.

Eliza had played like a princess and the title was duly won. But all the credit went to Huddle: "You Did It!" The partnership breaks up, leaving him to realize sadly: "I've grown accustomed to her game." But she finds that playing once again with her mother at the local club is intolerable and quietly returns. Huddle brightens up, and plans more hard work before the next Nationals.

January 3, 1982

CHAPTER 8
FREAKS

I cannot think of any bridge book that gives more than a passing mention to freak deals. Authors tend to suppose that the improbable can be ignored. But they do happen, and there is a guideline which is given in the first deal of this chapter. (See also the deal on page 133.)

All but one of these deals are true freaks in which one player has two voids. In the exception, there is "only" a nine-card suit. Several of them have results which are just about as improbable as the hands themselves.

WEIRD, WILD, BUT NOT DULL

Most players go through a lifetime without ever picking up a hand with 9-4-0-0 distribution, which they can expect ten times in a million deals.

If they do get such a hand, the bidding is likely to be dramatic but the play trivial: The more freakish the distribution, the less likely the play will present problems.

This rare parlay did develop during an early round of the 1981 Grand National team championship. Both South players gulped a little when they inspected their thirteen red cards, and when the deal was over, both pairs of defenders were swathed in guilty gloom.

When holding a totally freak hand with twelve or thirteen cards in two suits, the important thing is to be declarer. The level of the final contract is much less significant. So both South players bid six diamonds over four spades and were ready to bid seven diamonds if necessary.

In one case, as shown, seven diamonds was bid after North doubled. In the other, North boldly raised to seven diamonds over six spades. In view of the vulnerability, he no doubt expected his opponents to save in seven spades to insure themselves against a bad result.

Nobody chose to save in seven spades, a decision that was right in theory but wrong in practice. Both West players led a spade, and both South players ruffed and ran all their trumps. They could, of course, have maneuvered to discard one heart on the club ace, but that would have been foolish play: It would then have been obvious to the defenders that hearts was the suit they had to protect.

As it was, both West players went astray by unguarding hearts in order to cling to clubs. The grand slam was made, but neither side gained points.

"If I knew you were going to misdefend," grumbled East, "I would have saved in seven spades. That is down only 700, for I can pitch a club on a heart winner eventually."

"Your fault, not mine," retorted West. "If you had thrown both your clubs, I would have known to keep hearts. If you had thrown the six and eight of hearts, I would have known to keep hearts. Throwing spades told me nothing, and I had to allow for the possibility that you had the heart king."

April 11, 1981

NORTH
- ♠ 8 7 4
- ♡ 10 9 5 2
- ◇ Q
- ♣ A Q 8 6 4

WEST
- ♠ J 9 2
- ♡ Q J 4
- ◇ 6
- ♣ K J 10 7 5 2

EAST (D)
- ♠ A K Q 10 6 5 3
- ♡ 8 6
- ◇ 8 3
- ♣ 9 3

SOUTH
- ♠ —
- ♡ A K 7 3
- ◇ A K J 10 9 7 5 4 2
- ♣ —

North and South were vulnerable.
The bidding:

East	South	West	North
4 ♠	6 ◇	6 ♠	Dbl.
Pass	7 ◇	Pass	Pass
Pass			

West led the spade two.

ANYONE GOT A CALCULATOR

The most freakish deal from a regional tournament is shown in the diagram. This was a midnight game played with a fast time limit: five minutes a deal instead of the normal seven and a half minutes. It provides a good illustration of the bidding technique called for when holding a strong two-suited hand after an opponent has opened pre-emptively.

After West had opened with four spades, North not unnaturally fell in love with his hand. By bidding four notrump, a takeout request, and then diamonds at the six level, he showed a powerful hand with both red suits.

South converted to hearts and North pressed on to seven hearts. All he needed was to find South with four hearts, including the king.

Having the courage of his convictions, he redoubled when West made a dubious double. Great caution should be exercised in doubling a freely bid slam contract unless the doubler wishes to convey a lead-directing message.

If North had been the declarer, as he would have been after a normal auction, the double by West would be Lightner, asking for an unusual lead. This would help East to hit on the killing diamond opening that would give his partner a ruff.

But the serendipitous bidding had steered the contract into the South hand, from which position the grand slam was unbeatable. Perhaps West had forgotten that he was on lead. He put the club ace on the table, which was ruffed in the dummy.

Most of the allotted five minutes had been consumed by the auction, but South made no mistake in the play. He cashed the king–ace of hearts and began diamonds. West was unable to ruff, so it was a simple matter to ruff out East's diamond queen with the declarer's last trump.

Dummy was re-entered with a club ruff to draw the last trump, and the diamond suit scored all the remaining tricks.

At 2 A.M., with limited time, it was not easy to work out the score. The answer turned out to be 2,890, and West had reason to regret that he had not sacrificed in seven spades, losing a mere 500 points.

August 13, 1979

90

NORTH
- ♠ —
- ♡ A Q 8 6 5
- ◇ A K J 10 7 6 3 2
- ♣ —

WEST (D)
- ♠ K J 10 9 8 6 4 2
- ♡ 10 4
- ◇ —
- ♣ A 7 4

EAST
- ♠ 7 3
- ♡ J 9 2
- ◇ Q 9 8 5
- ♣ K Q 6 2

SOUTH
- ♠ A Q 5
- ♡ K 7 3
- ◇ 4
- ♣ J 10 9 8 5 3

North and South were vulnerable.
The bidding:

West	North	East	South
4 ♠	4 NT	Pass	6 ♣
Pass	6 ◇	Pass	6 ♡
Pass	7 ♡	Pass	Pass
Dbl.	Redbl.	Pass	Pass
Pass			

West led the club ace.

WHEN "PUSH" WAS THE UNEXPECTED REPLY

For no very good reason the word "push" has a colloquial bridge meaning. When teams are comparing scores, "push" indicates that no points have changed hands. The players then push on to the next deal.

The most unusual "push" of 1984 was surely the one resulting from the diagramed deal. It occurred in a Regional Swiss Teams in Cherry Hill, New Jersey, and East and West were Eileen Brenner of Livingston, New Jersey, and Dr. Michael Pickert, a dentist from West Orange, New Jersey.

North should perhaps have contented himself with a one-heart opening, but chose two clubs. He was relying on distributional power rather than high-card strength for his opening, a tactic that he was to regret.

East crowded the auction with a jump to four spades, and West cooperated by jumping to six spades when South inquired about aces. North–South had no clear agreement about how to deal with this situation, and were left in confusion.

North could not bring himself to pass, leaving his heart suit unbid. When he later doubled seven spades, which would have failed by three or four tricks for a small penalty, South overruled him. He could not believe that North had opened two clubs without two aces, so he tried seven notrump.

West doubled with confidence and collected 2,000 points.

When it came time to compare scores with their teammates, Miss Brenner and Dr. Pickert proudly announced: "Plus 2,000."

"Push," was the totally unexpected reply.

August 21, 1984

NORTH (D)
♠ K
♡ A K Q J 10 8 7 6 4
♢ K 3
♣ 6

WEST
♠ A 10 4 2
♡ 9 3 2
♢ 8 7 2
♣ 9 4 3

EAST
♠ Q J 9 7 6 5 3
♡ —
♢ 6
♣ Q J 10 8 5

SOUTH
♠ 8
♡ 5
♢ A Q J 10 9 5 4
♣ A K 7 2

North and South were vulnerable.
The bidding:

North	East	South	West
2 ♣	4 ♠	4 NT	6 ♠
7 ♡	Pass	Pass	7 ♠
Dbl.	Pass	7 NT	Dbl.
Pass	Pass	Pass	

West led the spade ace.

NO LEAD, NO PLAY, DOWN FIVE

For the connoisseur of bridge hands, finding a deal with a unique quality is a rare event. But the one shown in the diagram seems to represent a first-and-only in four different ways.

The deal was related by Pierre Jais, the great French expert. The hand was played in a rubber bridge game in Paris, and the hero was the late Ilyusha Babovich sitting South. It should be noted that the deal was a "goulash." In this form of the game, the cards are not shuffled and the cards are dealt in packets of three and four, resulting in wild distributions.

With no idea that he was looking at the hand of a lifetime, Babovich opened normally with one heart and heard his left-hand opponent overcall with one spade. His partner responded with two diamonds, and his right-hand opponent made an electrifying jump to six spades.

Babovich naturally doubled, but had to reconsider when East redoubled. East was an expert not given to excessive optimism, and if he redoubled it was because he felt confident that the slam would make. South was prepared to believe him, and, therefore, retreated to seven diamonds. This contract would have been down two, but East was not satisfied. He persevered to seven spades, and South again doubled. To South's amazement, East redoubled again.

East must think he can make seven spades, concluded South, and must, therefore, have an extraordinary hand. There is only one hand that could possibly justify East's bidding, thought South, and he knew what it was.

There was only one place to go from seven spades redoubled, and South went to it. He bid seven notrump as a save, knowing that his partner would be void in the opponents' suit. West doubled with some confidence, but before he could lead Babovich had something to say.

Leaning toward East, he announced confidentially: "You have five spades and eight hearts to king-jack-ten-nine-eight." Then turning to West, who had the spade ace half out of his hand, he announced: "No lead. Down five. 900."

And so it was. His analysis was absolutely accurate, and seven spades redoubled would have succeeded. North would no doubt have led a diamond, which would have been ruffed in the dummy. A high spade would have been played revealing the trump situation, and the declarer would then have led a high heart. With the hearts marked with South by the opening bid, it would then have been an easy matter to remove the ace–queen by ruffing. The trump entries in the East hand would have proved just sufficient to make use of the established hearts after drawing trump.

Before making his final bid Babovich had to think carefully about the spot cards in the heart suit. If he had held the heart nine instead of the

94

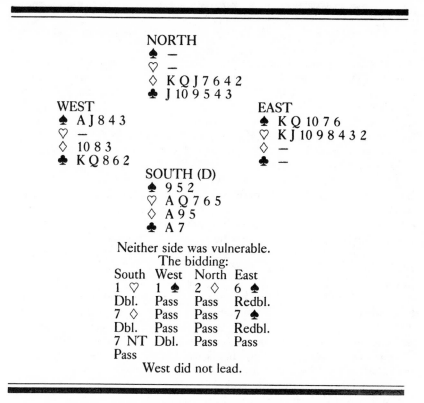

NORTH
♠ —
♡ —
◇ K Q J 7 6 4 2
♣ J 10 9 5 4 3

WEST
♠ A J 8 4 3
♡ —
◇ 10 8 3
♣ K Q 8 6 2

EAST
♠ K Q 10 7 6
♡ K J 10 9 8 4 3 2
◇ —
♣ —

SOUTH (D)
♠ 9 5 2
♡ A Q 7 6 5
◇ A 9 5
♣ A 7

Neither side was vulnerable.
The bidding:

South	West	North	East
1 ♡	1 ♠	2 ◇	6 ♠
Dbl.	Pass	Pass	Redbl.
7 ◇	Pass	Pass	7 ♠
Dbl.	Pass	Pass	Redbl.
7 NT	Dbl.	Pass	Pass
Pass			

West did not lead.

seven, he would have been willing to defend seven spades redoubled. Imagine that the nine and seven of hearts are transposed in the diagram, and that a diamond is led against seven spades redoubled. The contract can be made if West plays hearts immediately from the dummy, ruffing three times in the closed hand.

In practice, however, West would not make this play, for it would lose the grand slam if the spades divided 2-1. He would no doubt play one high trump at the second trick and can then no longer maneuver to establish the hearts.

And now for the four unique features of this deal:

It has surely never happened before that a player has correctly sacrificed in seven notrump when he held three aces; that a player has recognized in the bidding the crucial importance of a nine spot and has made a decision at the slam level based on it; that a player has turned to an opponent after the auction and accurately described his hand; and that a declarer has claimed a five-trick defeat in a slam before the opening lead has been made.

June 20, 1971

BIDDING A THREE-IN-TEN-MILLION HAND

It is safe to assume that a player who claims to have held a thirteen-card suit has either been the victim of a practical joke or is stretching the truth. Such a hand will occur about once in a hundred billion deals. The practical limit, without straining credibility, is an eleven-card suit, which should occur three times in ten million deals. This seems to have happened just once in international play—in 1961 in Sao Paulo. A local team representing Brazil was contending with the French international team, which was en route to the world championship in Buenos Aires.

The time was 2 A.M., almost at the end of the match, and René Bacherich of Lille, a small methodical man who had helped France win two world titles, dealt himself the staggering array of hearts shown in the diagram. No bid seemed quite right for this weird collection and he chose to pass, knowing, of course, that he would have another chance.

After a pass from East, South made a strong artificial forcing bid of two clubs. When West overcalled two spades, North made a spectacular jump to seven hearts. This was courageous but not unreasonable. He was, in effect, betting that his partner's strong opening included the heart king and the club ace, but he had extra chances. If the heart king was missing, it might not score a trick—in fact, the odds were substantially against both missing hearts being held by one opponent. And if the club ace was missing, the opponents would have to grab it at the first trick, before any discards could be taken.

This may be the first time a player has ever passed on the first round and jumped from two to seven on the second. This action took East by surprise, and he considered whether to sacrifice in seven spades. He reasoned, however, that North's bid must be a gambling effort, and he did not wish to sacrifice against a grand slam that was going to fail.

It is easy to see that seven spades is a sound sacrifice against seven hearts: Clearly it is better to be penalized 1,400 points than to have the opponents score 2,210. And when the bidding came around to West he duly bid seven spades, enraging South.

The South player, Claude Deruy, was a bailiff by profession, and he felt an urge to arrest West for improper conduct. His view was that East's hesitation over seven hearts had implied the possibility of a sacrifice in seven spades, and that West was taking advantage of information he was not entitled to.

Tournament committees often argue this sort of thing at length, but no committee was available on this occasion. And the bidding was not over. In a cold fury, Deruy bid seven notrump, an expensive way to vent his feelings. After the opening lead of the spade king he achieved the dubious immortality of going down 2,000 points in a voluntarily bid grand slam.

The proceedings, when the hand was replayed, were also remarkable.

```
                    NORTH (D)
                    ♠ —
                    ♡ A Q 10 9 8 7 6 5 4 3 2
                    ◇ —
                    ♣ K 4
WEST                                        EAST
♠ K Q 10 6 5 4 3                            ♠ A J 9 8 7 2
♡ —                                         ♡ —
◇ 7 6                                        ◇ 5 4 3 2
♣ J 10 8 6                                   ♣ 9 7 5
                    SOUTH
                    ♠ —
                    ♡ K J
                    ◇ A K Q J 10 9 8
                    ♣ A Q 3 2
```

Both sides were vulnerable.
The bidding:

North	East	South	West
Pass	Pass	2 ♣	2 ♠
7 ♡	Pass	Pass	7 ♠
Pass	Pass	7 NT	Dbl.
Pass	Pass	Pass	

West led the spade king.

Again the opening bid was two clubs, but this time by North. This was perhaps the only time in team play that a hand had been judged to be worth a game-forcing opening in one room, and a pass in the other. The French East, Roger Trézel, ventured a psychic overcall of two hearts with unfortunate results; North–South brushed aside the psychic and bid their way to seven hearts, while East–West never got around to bidding spades and so missed the profitable sacrifice.

The total swing in favor of the Brazilians was 4,210 points, or 25 international match points, the maximum possible. This record will never be equaled, because the scale was amended in the following year, and the maximum is now 24.

Deruy had two small crumbs of comfort to offset the publicity which his bid received throughout the bridge world. If he had not bid seven notrump but instead had doubled seven spades, his team would still have lost 14 match points. And even as it was, France won the match.

October 31, 1971

CHAPTER 9
TO EUROPE AND BACK

We start this chapter in a "Hungarian" bridge club. The Hungarian capital is Budapest, which was the scene of the first world championship. The star of the winning Austrian team on that occasion was Karl Schneider, a legendary cardplayer. Next we visit Melia, Spain, for a tournament appearance by one of the world's great actors, Omar Sharif. We return across the Atlantic on the luxury liner *Queen Elizabeth* II, and in Washington, D.C., find a Supreme Court jurist who is also a tournament bridge player.

HUNGARY FOR POINTS

The decision of George Bernard Shaw to make the egregious Zoltan Karpathy what Alan Jay Lerner later described as "a hairy hound from Budapest" undoubtedly did some harm to the image of the Hungarian people.

But it did emphasize their talent for languages and their ability to blend readily with other races. This has been noticeable in the world of bridge, for at least six other countries have been represented in international competition by Hungarians.

While some Hungarians are successful tournament competitors, others prefer the more peaceful battles of the rubber bridge table. Among the latter is Joseph Ivany of Huntington Station, Long Island, who learned the game in his native land four decades ago. On the diagramed deal, played at the Midway Club in Forest Hills, Queens, he had the distinct pleasure of occupying the South seat.

An opening four-club bid is usually based on a strong eight-card suit, a standard that the South hand does not meet. But the vulnerability was favorable, and Ivany took the plunge. This excited North, who chose to inquire for aces over West's four-heart bid. As the sequel demonstrated, East would have been wise to bid five diamonds as a lead-directing move rather than raise hearts immediately.

An opening pre-emptive bid sometimes goads the other players into wild excesses and did so here. West carried on to six hearts, which could have been doubled and defeated by three tricks. But North had made up his mind that he was going to play in clubs at any level and he bid a grand slam. Not unnaturally, East doubled.

North's redouble of seven clubs was either lunatic or genius. One might suspect the former, but the result suggests the latter. North may have been trying to scare his opponents into seven hearts, or he may have foreseen the result.

West knew that his partner wanted a lead other than hearts, but he could not decide whether to lead spades or diamonds. After considerable agony, he picked a spade, and that was wrong. South won in dummy and played another high spade, throwing his heart loser. He ruffed a spade and had no difficulty making the rest of the tricks. After the missing trump had been removed, dummy's spade winners provided discards for three losing diamonds in the closed hand.

The opening lead had swung the equivalent of 2,510 points, and East was boiling mad. But instead of screaming at his partner he should have apologized for his failure to bid five diamonds.

June 10, 1982

                    NORTH
                    ♠ A K 9 8 7 3
                    ♡ 5 2
                    ◇ 6
                    ♣ A Q J 2
WEST   EAST
♠ J 6 5   ♠ Q 10 2
♡ A K J 9 8 6 3   ♡ Q 10 4
◇ J 5 4   ◇ A K 10 9 7 2
♣ —   ♣ 3
                    SOUTH (D)
                    ♠ 4
                    ♡ 7
                    ◇ Q 8 3
                    ♣ K 10 9 8 7 6 5 4

East and West were vulnerable.
                The bidding:
    South   West   North East
    4 ♣   4 ♡   4 NT   5 ♡
    Pass   6 ♡   7 ♣   Dbl.
    Pass   Pass   Redbl. Pass
    Pass   Pass
    West led the spade five.

A Farsighted Claim

One of the most famous players in the history of the game, Karl Schneider, died in Vienna at the age of seventy-four in 1977. Before his retirement through ill health in the fifties, he was known as a player of the highest class, although his bidding methods seemed a trifle primitive to the scientists.

The high point of his career came in 1937, when he and his partner, Hans Jellinek, were the star pair of a young Austrian team that won the first world team championship, defeating Ely Culbertson's foursome in the final.

In the diagramed deal Schneider held the South hand and opened with two clubs. When West overcalled two spades, East tried a little nonsense by bidding two notrump, keeping his spade suit in reserve. He was trying to discourage South from bidding a slam, but Schneider brushed this aside and eventually jumped to seven clubs.

There was no guarantee that that contract would succeed. Even six clubs might fail if North could not control the third round of either red suit. But the grand slam was a fair gamble. If dummy produced Q-J-x-x in either red suit, it would be a laydown, and even if the slam was due to fail there was a fair chance that East–West would decide to save in seven spades.

When West led the spade king, Schneider no doubt regretted that he had not been content to bid six clubs. If dummy's four-card length had been in the suit with the queen, there would have been an obvious chance of a three-three break. As it was, it might seem that there was no escape from a diamond loser.

However, Schneider saw that he could make use of dummy's spade queen, superficially a useless card. He ruffed the spade ace, drew trumps in two rounds, and announced that he would make the grand slam if West held more than three diamonds. The opponents not unnaturally asked him to demonstrate, so he ran all his trumps to produce this position:

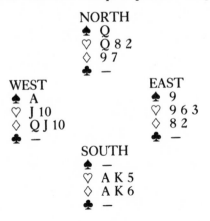

NORTH
♠ Q
♡ Q 8 2
♢ 9 7
♣ —

WEST
♠ A
♡ J 10
♢ Q J 10
♣ —

EAST
♠ 9
♡ 9 6 3
♢ 8 2
♣ —

SOUTH
♠ —
♡ A K 5
♢ A K 6
♣ —

NORTH
- ♠ Q 4
- ♡ Q 8 2
- ◇ 9 7 4 3
- ♣ J 10 9 6

WEST
- ♠ A K J 10 5
- ♡ J 10 7 4
- ◇ Q J 10 5
- ♣ —

EAST
- ♠ 9 8 7 6 3 2
- ♡ 9 6 3
- ◇ 8 2
- ♣ 8 4

SOUTH (D)
- ♠ —
- ♡ A K 5
- ◇ A K 6
- ♣ A K Q 7 5 3 2

Both sides were vulnerable.
The bidding:

South	West	North	East
2 ♣	2 ♠	Pass	2 NT
4 ♣	Pass	5 ♣	5 ♠
7 ♣	Pass	Pass	Pass

West led the spade king.

Now the A–K–Q of hearts crushed West, who had to save his spade ace. When he threw a diamond, the diamond six won the last trick in the closed hand.

September 14, 1977

Sharif the Playmaker

Omar Sharif's heavy acting schedule didn't stop him from attending a few European tournaments during 1974. He had a rare technical triumph on the diagramed deal played in the Melia Festival in Spain.

Sharif as South opened one notrump, and his partner, Paul Chemla, jumped to three spades. The partnership was using the weak notrump, and since South had a maximum, he endeavored to show this by a cue-bid of four diamonds. This implied a spade fit and a hand suitable for slam.

North then drove the bidding to the seven-level and, after finding out about aces and kings, chose to play in notrump rather than spades for match-point reasons. Sharif was none too sure about the wisdom of this decision when the dummy appeared. There were only twelve sure tricks available, and a spade contract would have offered more possibilities—an attempt to establish the club jack by a third-round ruff, for example.

West led the spade eight, fearing to lead away from the honors in the other suits, and Sharif studied his prospects. He could develop a simple squeeze against East if that player held the club queen and the diamond king: The plan would be to cash heart and club winners, and then lead all the spades.

A slightly better assumption, especially since West's spade lead suggested that he might have honors elsewhere, was that East held the club queen and West the diamond king. Then a double squeeze would operate, with hearts as the pivot suit. The procedure would be to cash the minor-suit winners followed by all the spades. If the cards were divided in the hoped-for fashion, neither defender would be able to preserve a heart guard.

Sharif chose to try for a third squeeze chance which was less obvious and more promising: the crisscross. He cashed his heart winners and one club winner before running spades, leaving the lead in dummy after the ninth trick with this position:

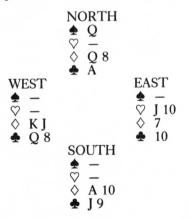

NORTH
♠ Q
♡ —
◇ Q 8
♣ A

WEST
♠ —
♡ —
◇ K J
♣ Q 8

EAST
♠ —
♡ J 10
◇ 7
♣ 10

SOUTH
♠ —
♡ —
◇ A 10
♣ J 9

```
                    NORTH
                    ♠ A Q J 10 7 6 3
                    ♡ 6 2
                    ◊ Q 8
                    ♣ A K
WEST                                    EAST
♠ 8                                     ♠ 4 2
♡ Q 8 3                                 ♡ J 10 7 4
◊ K J 9 6 4                             ◊ 7 5 3 2
♣ Q 8 7 6                               ♣ 10 3 2
                    SOUTH (D)
                    ♠ K 9 5
                    ♡ A K 9 5
                    ◊ A 10
                    ♣ J 9 5 4
```

Both sides were vulnerable.
The bidding:

South	West	North	East
1 NT	Pass	3 ♠	Pass
4 ◊	Pass	4 NT	Pass
5 ♡	Pass	5 NT	Pass
6 ♡	Pass	7 NT	Pass
Pass	Pass		

West led the spade eight.

When the last spade was led from the dummy, South threw the diamond ten, and West was caught helplessly in the crisscross fire. If he threw a diamond, South would play that suit and score the diamond queen for the thirteenth trick. And if he threw a club, the declarer would play that suit and score the club jack.

On a double-dummy basis the crisscross squeeze was due to succeed in two of the four possible distributions of the club queen and the diamond king. In practice the margin of superiority was somewhat less, since the declarer must read the distribution at the finish and an alert defender might succeed in confusing the issue by unguarding one of his honors at an early stage.

January 19, 1975

A Break in Concentration on the *QE*II

Shipboard games are perhaps more relaxed and sociable than any played on dry land. The players are more concerned about courtesy to the opponents and afternoon tea than they are about technical accuracy and acquiring top scores. The diagramed deal is an example of a *Queen Elizabeth* II card table drama.

Sitting North and South were David Enniskillen, a cosmopolitan Irish earl who does not use his title, and Carl Clopet of London. After passing a borderline hand, North had an interesting problem when his partner opened one diamond. There is no perfect response, but most experts would choose between one heart and three diamonds, or perhaps two hearts with a partnership agreement that this passed-hand jump shift promises a fit in opener's suit.

But North was determined to reach game, and, as no response was clearly forcing, he jumped all the way to five diamonds. This was not unreasonable and gave South the right impression. He wanted to use Blackwood, and, as four notrump was not available, he improvised with five notrump.

An expert would regard this as a grand slam force, asking for top honors in the trump suit, but such esoteric devices do not apply in mid-Atlantic. North interpreted his partner's unusual move correctly and bid six hearts to show two aces.

It was a distinct disappointment to South to find four hearts and two spades in the dummy. If North had held a 3-3-2-5 distribution, which would have seemed less attractive to him, the grand slam would have been a laydown, since dummy's heart losers would eventually be discarded on the K–Q of clubs.

As it was, a heart loser seemed inevitable. But Clopet did not despair. He won with the club ace in dummy and led the heart queen. East assumed that South held the A–J of hearts and made a slight error by playing low.

When the queen won, it was all over. And Clopet had become the first player ever to bring home a grand slam by taking a Chinese finesse in mid-Atlantic.

November 8, 1976

NORTH
♠ A 10
♡ Q 10 9 5
◇ J 7 6 4 3
♣ A J

WEST (D)
♠ K J 9 8 6 5
♡ J 2
◇ 5
♣ 10 9 5 3

EAST
♠ Q 7 4 2
♡ K 8 7 4 3
◇ 8
♣ 7 6 2

SOUTH
♠ 3
♡ A 6
◇ A K Q 10 9 2
♣ K Q 8 4

Neither side was vulnerable.
The bidding:

West	North	East	South
Pass	Pass	Pass	1 ◇
Pass	5 ◇	Pass	5 NT
Pass	6 ♡	Pass	7 ◇
Pass	Pass	Pass	

West led the club three.

JUSTICE STEVENS'S MOST MEMORABLE HAND

In the unlikely event that the Supreme Court ever has to decide a case involving bridge, Justice John Paul Stevens will be the resident expert. Justice Stevens has played the game for about fifty years and is a life master. He and his wife play in local duplicate games once or twice a month, and in sectional and regional championships whenever his work permits.

Justice Stevens's most memorable hand was a disaster. Many years ago he and his wife were competing in a parish tournament in Chicago. It was a rubber bridge knockout event, scored by total points, and they had reached the final. Judge Stevens, as he then was, sat West, and North was the parish priest, Monsignor Patrick Gleason, an excellent player.

The Stevens family was somewhat ahead in the score when this deal came along. South opened one spade, and North made a forcing jump to three spades, brushing aside the overcall of two hearts. South had an ideal hand for Blackwood and jumped to seven spades when his partner showed three aces.

The judge fingered his heart ace and looked suspiciously at both his opponents. South's final bid indicated that he believed that his partnership held four aces, but West was looking at one and there was no reason to suspect a defective deck.

After some thought, the judge reached a conclusion. No doubt North was void in hearts and had decided that this was the equivalent of an ace. In that case the lead of the heart ace would not help, and might establish the king in the South hand. Judge Stevens put a trump on the table and was surprised and hurt to find that dummy held two aces and no void.

South was also shaken to find that dummy had two aces, but recovered himself and brought home the grand slam. The overcall showed that West held the missing high cards, so he drew trumps and cashed all his remaining black-suit winners. When he led his last trump the position was:

```
                    NORTH
                    ♠ —
                    ♡ 7
                    ◇ A Q J
                    ♣ —
        WEST                    EAST
        ♠ —                     ♠ —
        ♡ A                     ♡ 9
        ◇ K 9 4                 ◇ 8 7 6
        ♣ —                     ♣ —
                    SOUTH
                    ♠ 7
                    ♡ K J
                    ◇ 2
                    ♣ —
```

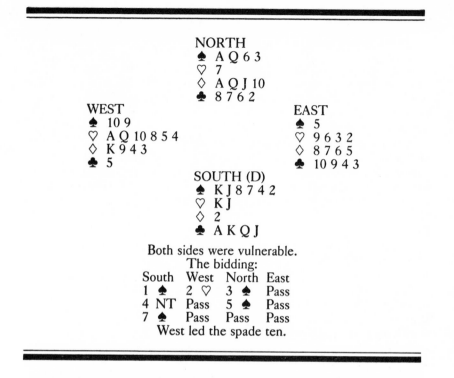

NORTH
♠ A Q 6 3
♡ 7
♢ A Q J 10
♣ 8 7 6 2

WEST
♠ 10 9
♡ A Q 10 8 5 4
♢ K 9 4 3
♣ 5

EAST
♠ 5
♡ 9 6 3 2
♢ 8 7 6 5
♣ 10 9 4 3

SOUTH (D)
♠ K J 8 7 4 2
♡ K J
♢ 2
♣ A K Q J

Both sides were vulnerable.
The bidding:

South	West	North	East
1 ♠	2 ♡	3 ♠	Pass
4 NT	Pass	5 ♣	Pass
7 ♠	Pass	Pass	Pass

West led the spade ten.

On the lead of the last trump, West was squeezed. In the faint hope that his partner held the heart king, he discarded the ace. South produced the heart king and finessed in diamonds to make the grand slam. Discarding a diamond would have been no better, for the diamond finesse would then have produced three tricks.

Many years later the judge and the priest, now old friends, discussed this memorable deal.

"To be deceived by a priest is something that still rankles after all this time," the judge said. "But tell me something: Did you lie deliberately about your aces, or did you make a mistake?"

"People confess things to me, not I to them," replied Monsignor Gleason. "But perhaps you would like to confess that you misdefended."

"That is true," Judge Stevens acknowledged. "I should have realized that leading the heart ace could hardly cost, for one discard in the North hand was unlikely to matter. And I now see that I could have beaten the hand by leading a diamond, breaking the squeeze. And I would have been the parish champion."

January 7, 1976

CONFUSIONS

Confusion at the bridge table is often a source of good copy for the bridge writer. Sometimes, it is true, some fabrication occurs. One of the deals in this chapter is fictional and another might be. The first one, however, is entirely factual. I was the suffering East player, and twenty-four years later it still hurts.

CLIMBING A MONKEY-PUZZLE TREE

A writer of bridge attempting to follow the customs of his profession is likely to be reminded of the Chile pine, a prickly tree of the genus *Araucaria*, by the deal shown.

Some of the customs are: Always make South the declarer, awkward in describing a team-of-four deal with two declarers in different positions; name at least one player, awkward when there is no hero; avoid naming those who wound up with guilt complexes, awkward when there are a number of red faces; and, if the writer is also a player, keep his name out of it.

All these journalistic problems combine to make this deal from the 1974 Grand National Team Championship in New York like the aforementioned monkey-puzzle tree, whose eccentric interlaced branches allegedly create difficulties for our simian cousins.

North and South had a strange bidding misunderstanding that requires explanation. They were using Jacoby transfer bids, so two spades by North promised both minor suits, and hinted at a slam. South could reasonably have bid six clubs directly, considering his remarkable minor-suit holdings which had to be ideal for slam purposes, but he bid a gentle three clubs hoping to reach seven clubs.

North bid a four clubs, hoping to rest in five clubs. But he had forgotten a partnership agreement, perhaps an unwise one, that four clubs would always be Gerber, asking for aces if the opening bid was notrump.

South dutifully showed two aces with four spades, and two kings when he heard five clubs, which North intended as a sign-off. He tried to sign off again, this time in six clubs, but South had other ideas.

North's unintentional inquiry for kings suggested grand slam possibilities and guaranteed that the partnership owned all the aces, just as a king inquiry would using regular Blackwood. So South decided that the diamond queen was a key card, filling a gap in the North hand, and carried on to seven clubs, making his partner shudder.

As West was looking at an ace he knew that something had gone wrong with the opponents' bidding. So he doubled, and proceeded to make an unfortunate lead decision. Instead of leading his spade ace, which might have run into a void in the dummy, he led the "safe" heart king and helped the declarer to bring home the doubled grand slam.

Even when he had escaped a spade lead, South was not feeling ecstatic. He had a theoretical 8 percent chance to make the contract by finding East with a doubleton diamond king but it was far more likely that West would produce the diamond king for a two-trick defeat.

Oddly enough, South would have been fairly happy to find West with the diamond king. He would then have suffered a small loss rather than a big one if the opposing North–South pair reached six clubs, failing by one trick, in the replay.

112

NORTH
- ♠ J
- ♡ A
- ◇ J 10 6 5 2
- ♣ 10 8 7 5 4 3

WEST
- ♠ A 10 8 6 5 3
- ♡ K Q
- ◇ 8 7 4 3
- ♣ 6

EAST
- ♠ Q 9 2
- ♡ J 10 9 7 6 4 3
- ◇ K 9
- ♣ Q

SOUTH (D)
- ♠ K 7 4
- ♡ 8 5 2
- ◇ A Q
- ♣ A K J 9 2

Both sides were vulnerable.
The bidding:

South	West	North	East
1 NT	Pass	2 ♠	Pass
3 ♣	Pass	4 ♣	Pass
4 ♠	Pass	5 ♣	Pass
5 ♠	Pass	6 ♣	Pass
7 ♣	Dbl.	Pass	Pass
Pass			

West led the heart king.

The actual distribution was a small miracle for South. He took the heart ace and finessed the diamond queen. Then he cashed the club ace, drawing trumps, and the diamond ace, collecting the king. Gulping slightly, he put his cards on the table, announcing that he would cross to dummy and throw his spades on the diamond winners. That made a rare score of 2,330 and generated considerable embarrassment, especially on the West side of the table.

In the replay, North–South did not manage to reach game, nor to find the club suit. They played in four diamonds, making an overtrick, and felt foolish. West at this table was Henry Bethe of New York, who did nothing in particular but rates a mention as the only mentionable player by journalistic convention. His team won 19 international match points on the deal, and West's failure to lead the spade ace against seven clubs cost 27 points.

May 21, 1978

Two Wrongs and a Right

It is well known that bridge books on bidding, like some wines, do not travel well: A treatise on a European bidding system is unlikely to find much of a sale on this side of the Atlantic. And the same is true of time barriers. American books on bidding written in the 1950s are of little interest today, and anything preceding World War II is virtually unreadable.

Books on play, however, travel much better through time and space. Some collections of hands emphasizing play are a permanent delight and belong on the shelves of any enthusiast. *Right Through the Pack* by the Hungarian analyst Robert Darvas and two books by S. J. Simon, all published in England about thirty years ago, are three examples.

A much older and rarer book first published in 1934 belongs in the same category and is perhaps the oldest bridge book still worth reading. It is *Odd Tricks* by Travis White, which was republished in 1978.

The author was an obscure Texan with a pleasant writing style. In the last deal of his book he featured himself, sitting East, as the innocent victim of a rare accident suffered by an opponent. The central figure was a retired army colonel who sat South and decided to open pre-emptively with four clubs, an entirely appropriate bid which would probably have ended the auction. But he inadvertently announced "four diamonds," and a prompt pass from West made it impossible for him to correct his call.

North should have suspected that something was wrong when he raised diamonds to the five-level and South bid six clubs: Any further bid by the pre-emptive bidder would be extraordinary, and an invitation to a grand slam unthinkable. But North stolidly reverted to diamonds at the six-level and again at the seven-level, showing no imagination.

White calls this second error by his opponents "expensive—not for them, but for us. Seven clubs cannot be made." His description of the sequel is worth quoting in full:

"South now perforce had to hold his peace. My partner opened the king of hearts, which was the correct lead. That is, I suppose it was correct—if you want to know the correct lead against a grand slam, don't ask me—consult a voodoo doctor. This apparently correct play capped the climax of a ludicrous situation by enabling South to make the accidental grand slam. The lead of any other suit would have defeated the bid.

"The colonel must have felt a bit weak in the knees; if the diamonds did not break three–three the set was going to be calamitous. But if shivers played about his backbone, he gave no sign; he stepped up to the precipice with all the dignity of a hotel doorman—and pushed us over the edge. Trumping the heart reduced his diamonds to two, leaving the dummy with two more than the closed hand. When three leads picked up

NORTH
- ♠ 9 8 7 4
- ♡ 6 5 3 2
- ◇ A K 5 3
- ♣ 2

WEST
- ♠ K J 5 3 2
- ♡ A K 9
- ◇ J 7 6
- ♣ 8 3

EAST
- ♠ A Q
- ♡ Q J 10 8 7 4
- ◇ 10 9 8
- ♣ 7 5

SOUTH (D)
- ♠ 10 6
- ♡ —
- ◇ Q 4 2
- ♣ A K Q J 10 9 6 4

Both sides were vulnerable.
The bidding:

South	West	North	East
4 ◇	Pass	5 ◇	Pass
6 ♣	Pass	6 ◇	Pass
7 ♣	Pass	7 ◇	Pass
Pass	Pass		

West led the heart king.

the adverse trumps he discarded his two spades on dummy's trumps, led a club and spread his hand. The grand slam cannot be made in clubs regardless of the lead because at that declaration only one spade can be discarded.

"Two errors in bidding by our opponents and correct defense by us combined to give them a vulnerable grand slam, which otherwise would have been neither bid nor made."

July 2, 1978

A Bad Agreement, Badly Applied

Those who object on principle to specialized conventions, and in particular to the weird agreements that some players favor, gain considerable satisfaction when the users fall flat on their faces as a result. But the theorists can usually demonstrate that the result is due to the misuse of the idea rather than to any fault in the theory.

It took major misjudgment in employing two bizarre agreements to give East–West their comeuppance on the diagramed deal, reported by Abe Paul in *Kibitzer,* a Canadian magazine.

South might have taken a shot at six spades as an opening bid, but he preferred to bid a gentle one spade. After action around the table he jumped to six spades over five clubs.

West doubled indignantly, perhaps forgetting that his partnership had agreed to use the negative slam double. When a save is plausible, a double shows no defensive tricks and encourages partner to bid.

The situation was not one in which this bizarre convention should be applied, but East thought it was. He bid seven clubs, a contract that would have failed by two tricks.

But South wrongly assumed that his opponents knew what they were doing. Perhaps seven clubs would make, and the penalty in seven spades was not likely to be great. He bid seven spades, so that the East–West misunderstanding seemed likely to increase the penalty.

Any normal defense beginning with a black-suit lead would have resulted in down four and a penalty of 1,100. West's decision to lead the diamond ace gave South some hope: Perhaps the spade nine would fall and the eight would be an entry to the dummy for heart discards on diamonds.

One would not expect it from an inspection of the diagram, but the spade nine did fall under the ace and North–South scored 2,470.

What had happened? East–West had another strange agreement: High-low in the trump suit shows no interest in ruffing. West applied this blindly, with catastrophic consequences.

Before the next deal East–West had some conversation. They agreed to abandon both the negative slam double and their high-low-in-trumps-denying-a-ruff.

October 24, 1983

NORTH
♠ 8 4
♡ 6 3
◇ K Q J 10 9 4 3
♣ 7 2

WEST
♠ 9 6
♡ A Q 10 7
◇ A 2
♣ A J 10 6 4

EAST
♠ 3
♡ 9 5
◇ 8 7 6 5
♣ K Q 9 8 5 3

SOUTH (D)
♠ A K Q J 10 7 5 2
♡ K J 8 4 2
◇ —
♣ —

Both sides were vulnerable.
The bidding:

South	West	North	East
1 ♠	Dbl.	3 ◇	5 ♣
6 ♠	Dbl.	Pass	7 ♣
7 ♠	Dbl.	Pass	Pass
Pass			

West led the diamond ace.

BIDDING WITH SCREENS

In the fifties an Italian, Mario Franco, devised a board which would stand diagonally on the card table, shielding each player from his partner and from one opponent. Long afterward, in 1974, experiments began in Europe and the United States. Since then screens have been standard in world team championships and in the late stages of American knockout team championships.

For many years it was normal for the bids to be announced by a neutral monitor at the corner of the table. Now, however, the authorities have adopted a sliding tray invented in Aruba. Each player, in his turn, places a bidding card on the tray and this becomes visible to the players on the other side of the screen when it slides underneath.

The controversy over the use of screens has generally overlooked one significant point. Not only do they have the obvious advantage of preventing cheating and any suspicion of cheating, but they have useful byproducts.

One of these is a sharp diminution in the ethical problems caused by hesitations: A hesitator can seldom be identified from the other side of the screen. Another is the disappearance of many infractions that disturb the normal course of the game.

Opening leads out of turn disappear, and so do bids out of turn, insufficient bids, accidental voice inflections, and slips of the tongue.

In the diagramed deal from the 1961 European championship, everyone was amused except East and West.

North and South were two young Italians who had learned to bid in English for the occasion. As the sequel showed, their mastery of this limited vocabulary was not total.

West pre-empted with three clubs, and North made a takeout double. He judged that his hand was worth a move toward slam when his partner jumped to four spades, and he made a cue-bid of five clubs.

South, an aggressive bidder, decided to accept the invitation and bid six spades. But in the heat of the moment he announced "seven spades." This surprised the three other players and himself when he realized what he had done. But he kept a straight face.

Against six spades, West would have led the club ace, but the bid of seven, made with confidence, convinced him that one of his opponents was void in clubs. In that case, the lead of the club ace was dangerous and might give away a trick.

Unaware of the accident—although the strangeness of a bid of four spades followed by a bid of seven might have alerted him—West led the spade jack. South drew trumps, ran his diamonds, and reverted to trumps. When he led his last trump, West was trying vainly to hold the club ace and guarded heart king. He discarded the heart nine, so South

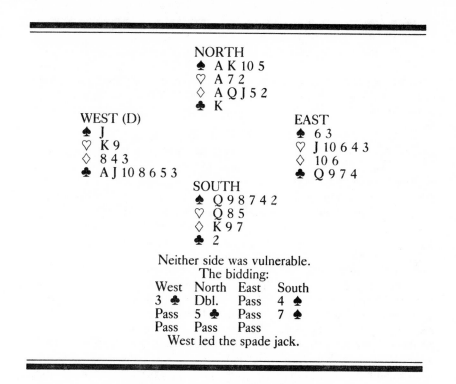

NORTH
♠ A K 10 5
♡ A 7 2
◇ A Q J 5 2
♣ K

WEST (D)
♠ J
♡ K 9
◇ 8 4 3
♣ A J 10 8 6 5 3

EAST
♠ 6 3
♡ J 10 6 4 3
◇ 10 6
♣ Q 9 7 4

SOUTH
♠ Q 9 8 7 4 2
♡ Q 8 5
◇ K 9 7
♣ 2

Neither side was vulnerable.
The bidding:

West	North	East	South
3 ♣	Dbl.	Pass	4 ♠
Pass	5 ♣	Pass	7 ♠
Pass	Pass	Pass	

West led the spade jack.

threw the club king from dummy and made the last trick with the heart queen to score the grand slam.

Writing about it many years later, East could finally see the funny side of it all. But it would not have happened if screens had been in use.

May 2, 1974

FEAR OF FALLING

A surprising number of bridge players suffer from acrophobia, or fear of heights. When the bidding reaches the seven-level, and thousands of points are at stake, they tend to get nervous and flustered, and lose their heads.

Home players are particularly subject to this malady and know it. Many of them never even venture to the seventh level, for fear of falling off the roof, and, as a result, miss many laydown grand slams.

Even experts sometimes suffer from this strange psychological ailment. Nearly twenty years ago, in a crucial European Championship match, the great Pietro Forquet of Italy bid a grand slam in a suit which was due to succeed. However, his partner converted to seven notrump, and the opponents cashed a bunch of tricks in a suit in which Forquet was void. With admirable self-control he said not a word to his partner, and, in spite of the catastrophe, they won the match.

In the diagramed example from the Spingold Knockout Teams at the Summer Nationals in New York in 1974, all four players, in varying degrees, displayed acrophobic symptoms. The bidding needs a good deal of interpretation. The one-club bid was not as natural as it seems: North–South were using a strong club system, and North promised at least 18 high-card points. East thought of jumping to three hearts, but saw that he was vulnerable and chose to pass. To his surprise South made the three-heart bid, which by partnership agreement was a transfer bid promising a long spade suit.

North dutifully bid three spades, and South had a problem. His best technical action was perhaps a cue-bid of four hearts followed by a jump to six spades, leaving North the option of continuing if he held first-round control of both minor suits. But there was a lurking danger in bidding four hearts—perhaps North would think that South had forgotten the system, and really had a long heart suit instead of spades.

South, therefore, tried Blackwood, not as a rule a desirable convention when holding a void suit. North showed two aces, and South was in trouble again. If the aces were in the minor suits, there was likely to be a grand slam. If not, even six could be in jeopardy.

Disregarding the faint possibility that six spades might fail, South came up with a pretty good answer. He made a cue-bid of six hearts, reckoning that if North held the heart ace he would recognize duplication in that suit and sign off in six spades.

Unfortunately, North was not quite sure what was going on. He considered three possibilities: One, that South had forgotten the system when he bid three hearts and wanted to play six hearts; two, that South held great length in both majors and was inviting North to choose between them; and three, the actual case, that South held long, strong spades with first-round control in hearts.

NORTH (D)
♠ 3
♡ Q J 6
◇ A K 5 2
♣ A K J 4 3

WEST
♠ 6 2
♡ A 4 2
◇ J 10 8 7 4
♣ 9 8 5

EAST
♠ 5
♡ K 10 9 8 7 5 3
◇ 9 3
♣ Q 10 2

SOUTH
♠ A K Q J 10 9 8 7 4
♡ —
◇ Q 6
♣ 7 6

Both sides were vulnerable.
The bidding:

North	East	South	West
1 ♣	Pass	3 ♡	Pass
3 ♠	Pass	4 NT	Pass
5 ♡	Pass	6 ♡	Pass
7 ♡	Pass	7 ♠	Dbl.
7 NT	Pass	Pass	Dbl.
Pass	Pass	Pass	

East led the heart eight.

Trying to cover all possibilities, North bid seven hearts, thus raising hopes in East's breast. But South converted to seven spades, and reached the right contract. If this had ended the auction, the deal would have been a standoff, since seven spades was reached in the replay. But now the trouble started.

West did not believe South's six-heart bid, and with North due to play the hand at seven spades, he made a Lightner double to ask for a lead of that suit. South was all set to redouble, but North panicked into seven notrump.

However, all was not over. West joyfully doubled seven notrump and was ready to lead the heart ace. But he made a slight error: He did not lead it quickly enough.

Like lightning, East worked out that his partner must be asking for a heart lead, and he put the heart eight on the table. Unfortunately, he had overlooked the Blackwood bid that served to make South declarer.

When advised by the tournament director of his four options, one of which was to bar the heart lead, South chose to accept the lead. Perhaps he thought that North must have the heart ace to bid seven notrump. Perhaps he was applying a theory that states that a lead out of turn should always be accepted because the player who does not know whose lead it is would not know what suit to lead either.

At any rate, West won the first trick with the heart ace, but East ducked the heart return. He was greedily hoping that his partner would gain the lead in spades to continue hearts, but this misdemeanor turned down two doubled and vulnerable to down one, 200 points instead of 500 points, costing him one trifling IMP.

September 8, 1974

CHAPTER 11
HAND OF A LIFETIME

Very few of the readers of this book will ever pick up a hand that seems likely to produce thirteen tricks with virtually no help from a partner. They can, however, console themselves with the thought that such hands often backfire. All the deals in this section are sad stories for the player who began the proceedings in a state of bliss. The last two, indeed, may rank among the saddest of all time—except for the opponents.

UNUSUAL USE FOR BLACKWOOD

To pick up the hand of a lifetime and wind up with a minus score is a deflating experience for anyone, but the ignominy increases substantially if partner is able to point out that a slightly more thoughtful approach to the problem would have left the partnership better off to the extent of about 2,700 points.

The diagramed deal was played many years ago in Asheville, North Carolina, and was recalled recently by J. W. Vandewart of that city. The player in the South seat was noted for making abrupt decisions, and opened the bidding confidently with seven spades.

He enjoyed the stunned silence that ensued around the table, but his enjoyment faded rapidly when everyone passed and West led the diamond jack. East ruffed and returned a club, and, by the time the smoke had cleared, the defense had taken the first five tricks, for a penalty of 500.

One would sympathize with South's opening bid at rubber bridge, for it seems quite reasonable, even if disastrous in the outcome, to try for 150 honors as well as the grand slam. But this was duplicate, so the honors did not count, and there was a positive advantage in playing seven notrump, for the extra 10 points, if North held the club ace.

Given these circumstances, the question arises how South should set about the bidding. If an opening four notrump bid is Blackwood, that bid can be used effectively. A variation popular in England is to use a four notrump opening to ask about particular aces. A five-club response still shows no aces, but other responses show the ace of the suit bid and five notrump promises two aces.

But without specific partnership agreement, such an action would be dangerous. Many players using traditional bidding methods would regard this bid as showing a balanced hand with about 28 high-card points. And a few experts use the bid nowadays to show a long minor suit with some slam interest.

So the safest procedure for South is to make a forcing opening at the two-level and eventually use Blackwood. When his partner admits to possession of an ace, seven notrump can be bid confidently.

"Why didn't you bid seven notrump?" demanded South in the postmortem, seeking to shift the responsibility for the disaster.

"Because you might have had a hand with two voids," retorted North. "You can think yourself lucky that the ruffs did not cost you anything. Since everybody else bid and made seven notrump, we'd have had the same bottom if you had made seven spades."

October 29, 1979

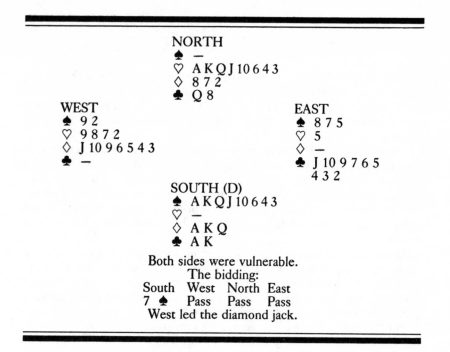

NORTH
♠ —
♡ A K Q J 10 6 4 3
◇ 8 7 2
♣ Q 8

WEST
♠ 9 2
♡ 9 8 7 2
◇ J 10 9 6 5 4 3
♣ —

EAST
♠ 8 7 5
♡ 5
◇ —
♣ J 10 9 7 6 5
4 3 2

SOUTH (D)
♠ A K Q J 10 6 4 3
♡ —
◇ A K Q
♣ A K

Both sides were vulnerable.
The bidding:

South	West	North	East
7 ♠	Pass	Pass	Pass

West led the diamond jack.

LISTENING TO TWO GRAND SLAMS

In New York City there are two types of club: the bridge club that has some social activity and the social club that has some bridge activity. Bridging the gap, and counting in both groups, is the prestigious Regency Whist Club, which has included many great players in its membership.

The Regency Whist team in inter-club competition was captained in the sixties by Raymond McGrover, a former President of the American Contract Bridge League and one of the game's leading lawmakers. On the diagramed deal, sitting South, he picked up the hand of a lifetime. His partner was Charles Lochridge, a brilliant player who won many titles in the 1930s and 1940s but confined himself to rubber bridge later in life.

Lochridge was reluctant to take part in the match because it clashed with a sporting event in which he was keenly interested. Finally, he consented to play on the understanding that he should be allowed to listen to a commentary on the world heavyweight championship bout, using a portable radio to be supplied by McGrover.

South's main concern was tactics: He wanted to play seven hearts with his freak hand without provoking the opponents into bidding seven spades. Therefore, he temporized with a cue-bid when East opened with three diamonds. He jumped to the grand slam on the next round, satisfied that his partner's spade bid had removed all danger of a seven-spade bid from the opposition.

But hands of a lifetime often prove disappointing, and this was no exception. West led the spade king, and after putting down the dummy, Lochridge gave his full attention to the radio.

South ruffed the opening lead and led the heart ace, prepared to claim the grand slam if both missing trumps appeared. The nine of hearts remained outstanding, and he had to choose between a technical and a practical line of play. The technical play was to lead three high clubs at once in the hope that West held at least three clubs: The club eight could then be ruffed in the dummy if West proved to have the suit stopped.

This would have failed as the cards lie, and McGrover played differently. He led out all his trumps in the hope that a defender with a club guard would discard in that suit. This put some pressure on East, but Dr. James Ducey, sitting in that position, correctly reasoned that South would not have bid seven hearts with a quick loser in diamonds. He discarded all his diamonds, therefore, and won the last trick with the club jack.

"Sorry, partner," said McGrover to his partner, whose thoughts were clearly elsewhere. "Perhaps I should not have bid it. But you had the worst possible club holding for me, and even as it is I had excellent chances."

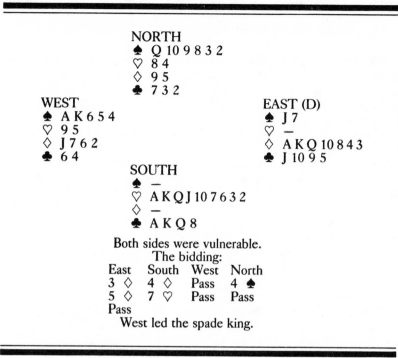

NORTH
♠ Q 10 9 8 3 2
♡ 8 4
♢ 9 5
♣ 7 3 2

WEST
♠ A K 6 5 4
♡ 9 5
♢ J 7 6 2
♣ 6 4

EAST (D)
♠ J 7
♡ —
♢ A K Q 10 8 4 3
♣ J 10 9 5

SOUTH
♠ —
♡ A K Q J 10 7 6 3 2
♢ —
♣ A K Q 8

Both sides were vulnerable.
The bidding:

East	South	West	North
3 ♢	4 ♢	Pass	4 ♠
5 ♢	7 ♡	Pass	Pass
Pass			

West led the spade king.

"Clay won by a knockout," announced Lochridge, switching off the radio. "I'd have shot you if you hadn't bid it," he added as an after-thought.

April 17, 1970

A Dream Hand Becomes a Nightmare

Bridge players sometimes dream about the game, and a really optimistic dreamer will find himself with the hand of a lifetime, a plausible opening bid of seven containing thirteen playing tricks. To add icing to the cake, the pleasure is prolonged by partner, who opens the bidding and shows great strength en route to the grand slam.

All this came true recently in real life, but the dream quickly turned to a nightmare.

North was considering shocking the table with an opening bid of seven. Equally dramatic, and slightly more efficient, would have been a forcing bid in spades followed by a bid of seven diamonds, asking for a choice at the level of seven.

North's reveries were disturbed when his partner opened the bidding with one club. He tried to show massive power and distribution by two successive jump shifts, naming his suits in a somewhat peculiar order. One spade and then seven diamonds would have conveyed the message in rather better fashion.

South took charge with Blackwood and plowed on to seven notrump when he found that the partnership held all the aces and kings. If West had led one of the declarer's suit, it would have been all over: South would have claimed. But after the lead of the diamond jack, he was dependent on the breaks. He needed spades 3-1 or 2-2, and they were, and he needed diamonds 3-2, but they were not.

Seven spades by North would have been a fraction better than seven notrump. By playing one round of trumps and then testing diamonds he could have guarded against the possibility that one defender held singletons in both key suits. But this would not have helped as the cards lie. The result would still have been down one.

It would not have been so easy to find a winning opening lead—spades or diamonds—if North had been declarer.

The moral of this sad story is this: If one leads against a grand slam in which there seems likely to be a massive number of tricks available to the declarer, try to give the lead to the more unbalanced of the two hands and you may create some entry problems.

September 6, 1980

NORTH
♠ A K Q 8 7 6 4
♡ —
◊ A K Q 9 4 3
♣ —

WEST
♠ 3 2
♡ 8 7 4
◊ J 10 8 5
♣ 10 7 4 2

EAST
♠ J 10
♡ J 9 6 5 3 2
◊ 7
♣ 9 8 6 3

SOUTH (D)
♠ 9 5
♡ A K Q 10
◊ 6 2
♣ A K Q J 5

Both sides were vulnerable.
The bidding:

South	West	North	East
1 ♣	Pass	2 ◊	Pass
2 ♡	Pass	3 ♠	Pass
4 NT	Pass	5 ♡	Pass
5 NT	Pass	6 ♡	Pass
7 NT	Pass	Pass	Pass

West led the diamond jack.

BIDDING TO THE EIGHT-LEVEL

Half a century ago black bridge players had virtually no opportunities to play in clubs and tournaments. They, therefore, formed their own organization; and although the discrimination that provoked their action withered away in the 1950s, the American Bridge Association has continued to flourish, and in 1983 it celebrated its fiftieth anniversary in New York.

A fascinating book, *A Nostalgic Reminiscence in the American Bridge Association*, was written for the occasion by Jim Garcia. In it he recalls the major personalities of the organization and gives notable hands played by them. The diagramed deal was played some thirty years ago at the 50th Street Club in Chicago and would surely rank among the most interesting freak deals of all time.

Starring in the South seat was Lola Scales, rated by many as the best woman A.B.A. player of that time. Playing the male lead in the West position was Frank Fail, known as "Buddy Boy." He had a reputation for subtle deception, and as the sequel demonstrates he liked to show off—especially, says Garcia, against Lola. Playing supporting roles were Dave Andrews, North, and Eloise Landry, East.

Fail began the proceedings with a cunning pass, confident that somebody would have enough length and strength in the major suits to open the bidding. He would then emerge quietly from the bushes, bidding diamonds as often as necessary in the expectation of being doubled. In attempting to carry out this plan, he slightly overstepped the bounds of legality.

Mrs. Scales, in the fourth seat, was also in the mood for a tactical underbid, which can often work well with an extreme freak hand. She contented herself with a gentle one spade rather than a forcing action. Fail, according to plan, bid two diamonds, but was surprised when he had to go to the seven-level on the next round. He was more surprised, and distinctly annoyed, when this did not buy the contract. South bid seven spades with reasonable hopes of success.

Whether from exasperation or a desire to show off, Fail now bid eight diamonds. When advised by the director that this illegal contribution was canceled, he protested: "But I can make eight diamonds." And so he could have done, if the requirement were to be no losers rather than fourteen winners.

The director also ruled, correctly as the law then read, that South could require or forbid an opening lead.

"Lead a spade," demanded South.

"Ain't got none," retorted Fail, which should have ended the matter.

"Lead a heart," tried South, carrying her rights further than the law allowed.

"Ain't got none of them either," was the triumphant answer.

"Then lead a club," was the final request. And West led the club ace, the card he would have led if left to his own devices. This was right in

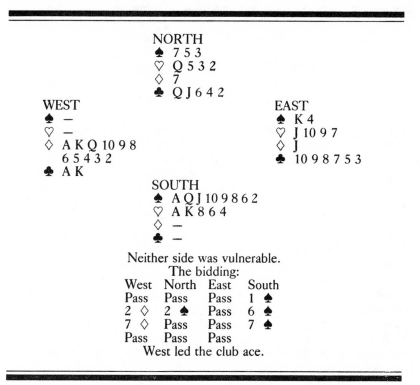

NORTH
♠ 7 5 3
♡ Q 5 3 2
◇ 7
♣ Q J 6 4 2

WEST
♠ —
♡ —
◇ A K Q 10 9 8
  6 5 4 3 2
♣ A K

EAST
♠ K 4
♡ J 10 9 7
◇ J
♣ 10 9 8 7 5 3

SOUTH
♠ A Q J 10 9 8 6 2
♡ A K 8 6 4
◇ —
♣ —

Neither side was vulnerable.
The bidding:

West	North	East	South
Pass	Pass	Pass	1 ♠
2 ◇	2 ♠	Pass	6 ♠
7 ◇	Pass	Pass	7 ♠
Pass	Pass	Pass	

West led the club ace.

theory but wrong in practice, for the implausible diamond lead would have beaten the grand slam.

It was now obvious that West held nothing but minor-suit cards and probably no losers. So South ruffed with the spade ten and led to the heart queen. She then led the spade seven and unblocked the spade six when East played low.

When this finesse predictably succeeded, she ruffed a club, removing the king. Then the ace of trumps collected the king, dummy was entered by leading the trump deuce to the five, and the heart losers were discarded on the club winners to make the grand slam.

The postmortem is not on record, but may have been something like this:

"I suppose I should have covered with the king," offered East, after thinking it over. "Then Lola is short an entry."

"I can do better," announced South, "by leading the five from the dummy. Then you can't beat me."

"I don't believe it," moaned West. "I had a grand slam in my own hand, and *they* made one."

July 31, 1983

OSWALD JACOBY BEATS

THE HAND OF A LIFETIME

Some sixty years ago a student at Columbia University became the youngest person ever to qualify as an actuary. Soon he became the enfant terrible of the bridge world and a master of many games.

Celebrating his eightieth birthday in December 1982, at his home in Dallas, Oswald Jacoby could look back on a quite remarkable life: the Culbertson–Lenz match, in which he walked out as Lenz's partner; a string of victories as a member of the Four Aces team, culminating in a victory in the first world team championship; intelligence duties in the Pacific in World War II; many more titles, until he was at the top of the masterpoint standings; and the privilege of leading an Aces team including his son, Jim, to victory in the 1970 World Championship.

Out of some quarter of a million deals he has played, Jacoby might well think that the one shown in the diagram is the most dramatic. He probably did not expect this, however, when his partner passed as dealer and he held a balanced 11 points.

However, West was looking at the hand of a lifetime. He could have taken a shot at seven hearts, but he did not want to push his opponents into seven spades. So he began with a cunning takeout double and bid his hearts gently at the five-level and the six-level.

This was good tactical bidding: The important thing for West was to be declarer, and the exact level was of secondary importance.

But at the six-level, West became foolishly greedy. When he was doubled he should have been satisfied with making a doubled slam with an overtrick. Instead he redoubled, and Jacoby worked out what was happening. He retreated to six spades, and, to West's considerable disappointment, carried on to seven spades over seven hearts.

West doubled in rage, and could have cashed two heart tricks. Not unnaturally, however, it seemed to him that the diamond ace was a better bet as an opening lead.

Jacoby had a good clue to the distribution, and he made no mistake. He made the key play of ruffing with the spade eight and led the spade four, finessing the six in his hand—a remarkable way to play the first round of trumps in a grand slam contract.

A diamond was ruffed with the spade jack, and the spade nine was finessed. The last diamond was ruffed with the last trump in dummy, and the closed hand was re-entered with the club ace.

The A-K of trumps drew the last two trumps from East, and five more club tricks gave Jacoby his doubled grand slam— certainly one for the memory book.

Sadly, Oswald Jacoby died in June 1984, at the age of eighty-one. But

NORTH (D)
♠ Q J 8 5 4
♡ 5 2
◇ —
♣ K Q J 10 9 8

WEST
♠ —
♡ A K Q 10 9 8 7 6
◇ A K Q 4 2
♣ —

EAST
♠ 10 7 3 2
♡ J
◇ J 9 8 7 3
♣ 4 3 2

SOUTH
♠ A K 9 6
♡ 4 3
◇ 10 6 5
♣ A 7 6 5

Both sides were vulnerable.
The bidding:

North	East	South	West
Pass	Pass	1 ♠	Dbl.
4 ♠	Pass	Pass	5 ♡
5 ♠	Pass	Pass	6 ♡
Pass	Pass	Dbl.	Redbl.
Pass	Pass	6 ♠	7 ♡
Pass	Pass	7 ♠	Dbl.
Pass	Pass	Pass	

West led the diamond ace.

seven months earlier he had set a record that may never be broken in any competitive activity. Four days before his eighty-first birthday he was a playing member of the team that won a major national championship, the Reisinger Board-a-Match Teams. He was already sick, but he was still a fighting competitor as he had been throughout his life.

December 8, 1982